AUTHOR 101

Praises for

AUTHOR 101
The Insider's Guide to Publishing
From Proposal to Bestseller

"I know you are thinking about Author 101. All I have to say is that I am a product of it. Really, I am a product of Rick Frishman. If I had not met Rick, I would not have done my book the way I did, and I probably would not have gotten published. I probably never would have made it to #1 on *New York Times*, #1 on *The Wall Street Journal*, Barnes and Noble, and Amazon. As for Author 101, there are not really any book events that can train you how to create a book proposal, how to get an agent, how to talk to an agent, how to find a publisher or how to sell a book. If you want to find a self-publisher, what are the strategies that work today to write a great book and promote it. Author 101 gives you all you need to know to become a best-selling author in the publishing world. Rick has guided me and I know he can guide you."

Brendon Burchard, #1 *New York Times* Best-Selling Author

www.Brendonburchard.com

"It has been absolutely amazing to be here at Author 101 University. Everything from mindsets, to strategies, to building a book, selling a book, and marketing a book. It is a all here. It has been an exciting event. If you are even thinking of being an author, or you are an author and you want to take it to the next level, then this is the place to be."

John Assaraf, #1 Best-Selling Author, www.johnassaraf.com

"If you want to be a best-selling author, you need smart advice from top experts like Rick Frishman and Robyn Spizman. *Author 101: The Insider's Guide to Publishing From Proposal to Bestseller* is filled with the keys to your success. Buy this book and put it to use today. You just might be sitting on the next bestseller!"

Ken Blanchard, New York Times best-selling author,

The One Minute Manager

"Nobody knows how to publicize books better than Rick Frishman and Robyn Spizman. This terrific, information-packed book could be your ticket to the bestseller list."

Mark Victor Hansen, Co-creator of the *Chicken Soup for the Soul* series

"A wealth of advice for every aspiring author determined to make their masterpiece stand out above the rest. Even after many years in this industry there's something new to be learned. *Author 101: The Insider's Guide to Publishing From Proposal to Bestseller* is a gold mine for those on both sides of the publishing door."

Grace Freedson, Literary agent

"*Author 101: The Insider's Guide to Publishing From Proposal to Bestseller* is loaded with inside information compiled by two experts and tons of publishing pros. A must for anyone who wants to get a book published."

Pamela K. Brodowsky, President International Literary Arts, coauthor of the *Staying Sane* series

"Where was this fabulous book when I had to write my first proposal? Finally, a straightforward guide that tells you exactly what to do, and why."

Bill Catlette, Coauthor *Contented Cows Give Better Milk*.

"I can't think of any better source of the latest 'how-to's' in the book proposal world. Your guides are masters—they've worn the hats of author and publicist and work closely with the major publishers. In your hands is the book that will shape the ideal proposal to sell your work."

Judith Briles, Author of *The Confidence Factor*

"Indispensable! The new bible on how to write book proposals. The clearest and most comprehensive book on book proposals. Does everything short of writing proposals for you!"

Jack O'Dwyer, Editor-in-Chief. O'Dwyer PR publications

"Rick and Robyn have created the clearest and most comprehensive book on book proposals. This book is extraordinary, and if you are an author, or aspiring to be one, this book is for you!"

Peggy McCall, Author of *The 8 Proven Secrets to SMART Success*

"Now you can stop toying with the idea of writing a bestseller—just get this book and follow it like a treasured recipe. Rick and Robyn have gathered the experts, cracked the code, and have brilliantly revealed all of the important secrets, tips and shortcuts in this book. If you're an author, this book is indispensable. Get it, read it, follow it."

Randy Gilbert, Founder of InsideSuccessRadio.com and cofounder of BestSellerU.com

"If you want to write a successful nonfiction book, you have to have a great platform. Rick and Robyn have done an amazing job of compiling one of the best books around on building a successful platform for your book."

Alex Carroll, Best-selling author and founder of www.RadioPublicity.com

"Rick and Robyn's *Author 101* book answers the pertinent questions that all writers and publishers need to know to travel the road to success."

Jerrold Jenkins, www.bookpublishing.com

"Rick and Robyn are the masters at teaching authors how to be SUCCESSFUL AUTHORS. Read this book and learn from the best."

Robin Sharma, Professional speaker and author of *The Monk Who Sold His Ferrari*

"*Author 101: The Insider's Guide to Publishing From Proposal to Bestseller* is what every aspiring author needs: a practical, easy-to-follow information-packed guide."

Steven Schragis, Founder of One Day University

"If you want to become a published author, the first step is buying Rick and Robyn's book. Loaded with practical, easy-to-follow insider advice... Highly recommended!"

Lloyd J. Jassin, Publishing attorney and author.

"Rick and Robyn show you how to get your foot in the door... Just as importantly, they tell you what not to do. This book should be on the desk of every aspiring writer."

Marion Gropen, Gropen Associates, Inc.

If there was an official list of books required of writers to read before publishing, then *Author 101: The Insider's Guide to Publishing From Proposal to Bestseller* should be at the top of that list! I couldn't help but think to myself as I read through the book, it doesn't just start with how to write a great book proposal (as the book title suggests), but begins with how to get started, knowing your audience and developing a platform. Many folks can talk about publishing a book successfully, but Rick Frishman and Robyn Spizman actually break it down and show you how. If you want to go from book idea to bestselling author, don't just read this book, study it and put it into action!"

Eric V. Van Der Hope, International Bestselling Author of *Mastering Niche Marketing*

AUTHOR 101

The Insider's Guide to Publishing
From Proposal to Bestseller

RICK FRISHMAN and
ROBYN SPIZMAN
With Mark Steisel & Justin Spizman

NEW YORK

AUTHOR 101
The Insider's Guide to Publishing From Proposal to Bestseller

© 2015 **RICK FRISHMAN** and **ROBYN SPIZMAN**.

Published in New York, New York, by Morgan James Publishing. Morgan James and The Entrepreneurial Publisher are trademarks of Morgan James, LLC. www.MorganJamesPublishing.com

The Morgan James Speakers Group can bring authors to your live event. For more information or to book an event visit The Morgan James Speakers Group at www.TheMorganJamesSpeakersGroup.com.

Author 101™ is a registered trademark.

ISBN 978-1-63047-375-4 paperback
ISBN 978-1-63047-376-1 eBook
ISBN 978-1-63047-377-8 hardcover
Library of Congress Control Number: 2014946130

A free eBook edition is available with the purchase of this print book.

CLEARLY PRINT YOUR NAME ABOVE IN UPPER CASE

Instructions to claim your free eBook edition:
1. Download the BitLit app for Android or iOS
2. Write your name in **UPPER CASE** on the line
3. Use the BitLit app to submit a photo
4. Download your eBook to any device

Cover Design by:
Rachel Lopez
www.r2cdesign.com

Interior Design by:
Bonnie Bushman
bonnie@caboodlegraphics.com

Photo of Robyn Spizman:
Keiko Guest Photography

In an effort to support local communities, raise awareness and funds, Morgan James Publishing donates a percentage of all book sales for the life of each book to Habitat for Humanity Peninsula and Greater Williamsburg.

Get involved today, visit
www.MorganJamesBuilds.com

Habitat for Humanity®
Peninsula and Greater Williamsburg
Building Partner

DEDICATION

All it takes to get a book published is getting one person to say yes. We dedicate this book to the editors, publishers, and individuals along the way who said yes to us and hopefully will say yes to you too.

To my wife, Robbi, with love and thanks.
—Rick Frishman

To my husband Ed! You make life a bestseller!
—Robyn Spizman

TABLE OF CONTENTS

FOREWORD

Have you ever wanted to write a book but didn't know how to get started? This is the most common problem that would-be authors have, and now there is a solution.

Rick Frishman and Robyn Spizman have put their many years of experience into this excellent book, *Author 101: The Insider's Guide to Publishing From Proposal to Bestseller* to give you a clear, comprehensive, and information-packed guide. It will show you how to get started and take you along, step-by-step, until your book is completed and ready for the publisher.

Rick and Robyn have brought together an all-star team of professional writers to show you exactly how to write a nonfiction book. In this single volume, Rick, Robyn, and their friends will take you through the process of writing a nonfiction book from the idea through to completion. You will learn how to plan the stages of writing the book, research the critical information, organize the information into logical chapters, and then write and edit it so that it reads well on the page. This book shows you straightforward and easily understood concepts and insider secrets that have taken them years to learn.

Over the years, I have written more than forty books and continue to publish top-selling books at the rate of four per year. My books have been translated into thirty-four languages and are sold in forty-seven countries. I know firsthand the importance of learning the writing process before beginning. I have read dozens of books and articles on "how to write a book," and this book, *Author 101: The Insider's Guide to Publishing From Proposal to Bestseller* is a summary of the best ideas ever discovered to help you become a published author.

Authoring a book is an extremely rewarding accomplishment; few experiences can match it. It can help you, your career, and thousands of readers. By sharing your ideas, insights, and information, you can help others all over the world.

Publishing your book can increase your visibility, establish you as an authority in your field, and enable you to meet and forge close relationships with other remarkably accomplished individuals. However, writing a book isn't easy. If it were, everyone would be doing it. Many people have been toying with the idea of writing a book for many years.

Writing a book cannot be done haphazardly. It takes lots of time, planning, work, discipline, and persistence. In addition, you need plenty of help and guidance, especially the first time, and that is what this book will give you. *Author 101: The Insider's Guide to Publishing From Proposal to Bestseller* explains exactly what you need to do to start, write, complete, and edit your book. It shows you what successful authors have done over the years.

Rick and Robyn know that every writer, book, and subject differs and that authors can take a variety of different approaches in creating nonfiction books. They also understand how necessary it is for your book to be an expression of your personal thoughts and observations, rather than just an imitation of some other author or book.

To help you write a book that will show you at your best, Rick and Robyn have enlisted the help of more than forty top authors to explain what has worked for them. They guide you through the multifaceted world of nonfiction books. The authors weave in a broad spectrum of advice from true professionals that you could not otherwise obtain.

What you will get in this wonderful book is a detailed roadmap for writing nonfiction, along with a selection of options that you can use. *Author 101: The Insider's Guide to Publishing From Proposal to Bestseller* will help you to choose the best path for you and avoid many of the pitfalls that have traditionally sabotaged would-be writers.

Read this book from cover to cover, and then read it again. Refer back to it often as you write your first book, and subsequent books. These ideas will put you on the high road to success as a published author.

Brian Tracy

www.briantracy.com

ACKNOWLEDGMENTS

Our warmest thanks to our many friends and gifted literary contacts whose help and wisdom made this book possible. When we asked them to help us, these friends consistently came through and shared their remarkable knowledge, experience, and insights with us. They selflessly took time from their busy schedules to help us and the readers of this book.

To all of the authors who are listed below, thank you for so generously sharing your time and expertise with us. Your knowledge, insights, and wisdom gave this book life. Your contributions will help many aspiring writers. We are extremely grateful for your help! The authors we interviewed for this book are:

Dr. Dan Baker

Jean-Noel Bassior

Arthur H. Bell

Peter Bowerman

Joseph Cardillo

Charles Cerami

Judi Culbertson

T. Harv Eker

Judy Ford

Lois P. Frankel, PhD

David Fryxell

Malcolm Gladwell

Gregory Godek

Seth Godin

Stedman Graham

Jeff Greenwald

Casey Hawley

Collins Hemingway

Alison James

Lloyd J. Jassin, Esq.

Tory Johnson

Guy Kawasaki

Theodore Kinni

Leonard Koren

Jay Conrad Levinson

Jennifer Block Martin

Louis Patler

Katherine Ramsland

Mary Roach

Al Ries

Laura Ries

Brad Schoenfeld

Daylle Deanna Schwartz

Dr. Brenda Shoshanna

Sara Slavin

Diane Shader Smith

Florence M. Stone

Stephen Yafa

Brian Tracy

Bill Gladstone

T Harv Eker

Peter Hoppenfeld

Richard Curtis

Ken Atchity

Mitch Albom

David Hancock

Terry Whalin

John Willig

Justin Spizman

John Asarraf

Brendon Burchard

Richard Narramore

Scott Hoffman

From Robyn: To my wonderful family—my husband, Ed. To Justin and Jaime, Dani and Bella, Ali and Marc, Michelle and Jeff and J.D., Alicia and Lee and Randi - You all fill my life with laughter and love. To my parents, Phyllis and Jack Freedman, who have always cheered me on to success. To my coauthor, Rick Frishman, who is genuinely one of the finest human beings on this planet. Thank you, Rick, for being such a remarkable friend and coauthor. And to the talented Mark Steisel, who is a total literary genius in our book! And to my son Justin Spizman for his outstanding efforts to update this book and make it happen. Justin—you are undeniably one of the finest writers we have ever known and we appreciate your non-stop support helping make the Author 101 series successful.

From Rick: The first thank-you goes to my wonderful coauthor, Robyn Spizman, whom I have known for over twenty years and who is one of the finest coauthors a guy could ask for.

Mark Steisel—your help and wisdom have been invaluable. Working with you has been a joy.

Justin Spizman—thank you so much for your willingness and efforts to help update this book. You are an extremely talented writer and it has been a pleasure working with you over the years.

I have to acknowledge Mike (Manny) Levine, who founded Planned Television Arts in 1962 and who was my mentor, and partner, for over eighteen years. Mike taught me that work has to be fun and meaningful and then the profits will follow.

To my friends Mark Victor Hansen and Jack Canfield. Making the journey with the two of you has been incredible, and your friendship and advice have been invaluable.

To Harvey Mackay, for the lessons about networking and for your amazing support. You are in a class of your own.

To my mother and father, for keeping me out of the fur business and helping me discover my own destiny. And to my brother Scott, who has always been there to support me in whatever I do.

To my children, Adam, Rachel, and Stephanie. Watching you grow into fine young individuals has been the highlight of my life. And to my wife, Robbi— you are my strength.

INTRODUCTION

The term *nonfiction books* covers a lot of ground. When we use the term, we're talking about a huge variety of books. And the books that are included under the umbrella of nonfiction can differ as greatly as day and night.

Nonfiction books have been written on virtually every imaginable subject, in every conceivable format, and by a wide spectrum of totally different authors. The category even includes titles on how to write nonfiction—and fiction.

To some readers, the term *nonfiction* may immediately bring to mind biographies, autobiographies, and memoirs. Others may think of historical, business, technological, and scientific books. They're all correct. The term also embraces how-to, instructional, or entertaining volumes on history, art, philosophy, psychology, health, travel, food, diet, exercise, and nutrition, to name just a few. And let's not forget textbooks, dictionaries, encyclopedias, almanacs, yearbooks, and workbooks, also nonfictional works.

Since the variety of nonfiction books can be so diverse, telling aspiring writers how to tackle nonfiction books is somewhat akin to suggesting how they should raise their children. While a handful of basic rules may exist, they're often obscured by an infinite number of theories, which don't always work. Plus, many terrific books have successfully broken the rules.

To compound the problem, when it comes to writing nonfiction, anyone who reads may feel qualified to speak as expert. People who rarely open a book—and would never dream of writing one—may not hesitate to tell you what you should write and exactly how you should write it. They may freely critique, criticize, and comment on your writing even though they've never seen it. All of this advice can cause writers to shut their ears and take cover, which can make the writing experience even more isolated.

Why This Book

As experienced writers, we've listened to everyone's suggestions and advice. Much of it we've even followed with varying degrees of success. We've read the top books on writing, and we attend major writing events like Author 101 University in Los Angeles, at which we frequently speak. Books and writing are not only our business; they're our passion. We know and hang out with leading authors, agents, editors, and publishing industry professionals. We constantly talk with them about writing, discussing problems and offering possible solutions.

Most people consider us writing and publishing insiders; we've been at it for years. We know books and writing well. Writing and promoting them are what we love, and people tell us that we do it excellently. In fact, they pay us for it. So we know the ropes, the rules, and the realities, as well as many of the major players. In the books we've written, we've broken many of the rules and created lots of new ones of our own.

You see, when it comes to writing, there are a number of ways you can go. Everyone seems to have his or her own special favorite, and he or she is usually happy to explain it to you. Unfortunately, what works for them, or everyone else, may not work for you. So you've got to find your own way.

We've found that there is no right way or wrong way to write successfully. Every writer must find his or her own direction and voice. Writing is more than just sitting down and stating what you know, think, feel, or observe. It's not just transcribing your speeches and presentations, or having someone write up your notes. Writing is a process of exploration. It requires you to think, feel, set goals (which will frequently change), and take chances. You must be organized and dedicated and you must persevere.

Although you always hear about the loneliness of writing, of authors sealing themselves off and writing until their fingers ache, books can't be written in isolation. You must read, gather information, and learn. Then you must organize that information and present it in a compelling manner that will hold readers' interest and make them want more.

To be a successful writer, you must take charge. You must take the helm, assume responsibility for your career, and move your writing in the direction you wish to pursue. To do so, you need to know the options that you can use to write your book. In this volume, we want to show you some of those routes, methods that worked for us and for other successful writers.

Instead of simply lecturing you on our theories, we decided instead to tell you how other successful writers have proceeded. So, we contacted scores of outstanding writers, many of who generously shared their insights and experiences with us. We made it a point to interview a wide variety of top professional writers, individuals who are dedicated to writing excellently; authors who have seriously thought, and often taught, about the art of writing. A number of the authors we interviewed have published dozens of books, while others have written only one or two. Our interview subjects also come from a disparate array of fields, which should provide you with varying points of view.

In many ways, this book is a survey of authors and their methods, a detailed description of how many writers work and their experiences. We decided to write this type of book in order to give you a buffet, a smorgasbord, of ideas that you can examine before you go to work. Which you use and how you use them, if you even do, is strictly up to you.

Our hope is that as you're reading this book, you will get a sense of what is involved in being an author, the steps you must take, the obstacles you may face, and the ways you can surmount those obstacles. From the material we present, we want you to visualize where you will sit, how you will conduct your research and write. We want you to imagine the filing system that you will create and how you will document and keep track of the information you collect. In other words, we want to take you through the book-writing experience and what you may have in store.

Enjoy this book, and we wish you the very best of luck with your writing.

Rick Frishman
www.Author101.com
Robyn Spizman
www.robynspizman.com

Chapter 1

SO WHAT ARE YOU GETTING INTO?

All the fun is in how you say a thing.
—Robert Frost

This chapter covers:

- Why Books Matter
- Learn about writing
- The elements of writing
- The elements of publishing
- Publishing is a business
- The platform requirement
- Self-publishing

Why Books Matter

Bill Gladstone, author of several best-selling novels and non-fiction titles as well as the literary agent for such luminaries as Eckhart Tolle, Neale Donald Walsch, Thom Hartmann, Jean Huston and Dr. Ervin Laszlo, discusses why books matter. He said, "I have always encouraged those who approach me to explore and develop their own writing talents. Sometimes this may lead to publication by a major publishing house, sometimes to an opportunity to self-publish and sometimes to a realization that the book that one is writing might be just for a private audience of one. Even if no one but you reads your book, you may have changed your own life in taking on and completing a book. Writing a book can be a cathartic experience that puts you in touch with a greater self-awareness than you could achieve any other way."

"But the personal benefits aside, books matter a great deal and here are the reasons why:

1. Books can be shared;
2. Books can create characters and experiences for readers that transport them to other worlds;
3. Books can teach us what it means to be fully human;
4. Books allow us to participate in collective discussions;
5. Books can present new ideas;
6. Books can be beautiful works of visual art;
7. Books can be read to children;
8. Books can be our legacy to future generations;
9. Books can allow us to travel throughout the universe without ever leaving home;
10. Books can make us laugh;
11. Books can move us to tears;
12. Books can create political movements;
13. Books can change society;
14. Books can create bridges that heal conflicts;
15. Books can challenge our intellect and imaginations;
16. Books can inspire us;
17. Books can make us better people;

18. Books can provide information that can save lives;
19. Books can change our mood;
20. Books can preserve our appreciation of historical events and times;
21. Books can challenge our creative efforts in whatever field we choose;
22. Books help us learn who we really are."

Books offer an amazing opportunity and medium to exchange information. They create relationships, form friendships, and promote growth. Specifically, non-fiction books offer the exciting opportunity to change and improve. Success is not only an art, but also an attainable trait. Non-fiction books are often the conduits to achieve your goals. Together, we will work to help you tap into your ideas, concepts, and dreams to help you help others make substantial differences in their lives.

Start writing; start now! Take your ideas, your thoughts, and the information you want to convey and put them on paper or on your computer because no one can read a book that exists solely in your head. Do it now.

We understand the intimidating nature of blank sheets of paper in front of you and how painful it can be to try to write. But do it. Force yourself. Do it now. Write anything, even if it feels empty, useless, or like total gibberish or nonsense. Start by putting something, anything, on the page. Don't criticize or judge what you write. Don't edit it, don't even read it; just write.

Write to get the feel of it, to get into the rhythm, the flow of writing. Writing has a musical component, a pulse that resonates in your head. When you're cooking, your writing takes on a distinct cadence and meter; it feels like a song in your mind. It may take a while to emerge, but as you're laboring, the tempo can sneak up on you and take you by surprise. Suddenly, you'll find yourself into it; your words materialize, make sense, and gracefully glide. It's almost as if they begin writing themselves, jumping out of your head and pulling you out of your self-consciousness, reluctance, and fear.

That rhythm is what writers work for, and so should you. It should be your target, your main objective. It tells you that you're on the right track, which means you've got something. It's like when you finally get the knack of skiing, dancing, or riding a bike. You get lost in it and a part of you lets go so that it becomes almost automatic, but another part—the writer part—magically takes over and seizes control.

When you don't feel the pulse, keep at it. Write until it comes, even if what you're writing feels like a total waste. Because the simple act of writing is never a waste. The mind sends ideas to your fingertips and they begin to come to life on paper or the computer screen in front of you. Force yourself to put words on the page, make it a crusade, keep your fingers moving, and write fast.

Try to write two or three pages, and after you've completed them, sit back and relax. Take time to refresh, recharge, and prepare to write more. Don't worry about the quality of your writing. Instead, think about how you felt. Did you feel the rhythm? Were you close? Read what you wrote, but don't be critical or severe. Search for hidden nuggets, little jewels that may be embedded in the mess. Look for ideas that you could develop to form the basis of your book.

Get it on paper! Write, write, write.

Learn about Writing

Writing a nonfiction book is a remarkably satisfying achievement; it can be one of the great highlights of your life. Learning how to write can be a journey in which you learn about yourself and uncover parts of you that you never knew existed. Learning to write can open up new and wonderful worlds from which you may never turn back.

Writing a nonfiction book is an accomplishment one many strive for, but few actually reach. The mere realization of just how much you know about a subject, how well you have explained it, and how your knowledge can help others is thrilling, especially when you see it in black and white. Being a published author will give you an elevated status and enhanced credibility; people will look at you differently, and it can enrich every aspect of your life. And we're here to help you achieve it; to help you join us on the bookshelves and even the bestseller lists.

But first—a brief word of warning:

No matter how bright you are, regardless of how much natural talent you may posses, you can't compete at the highest levels the very first time you try. It takes practice and hard work. When you write and try to publish a nonfiction book, you're playing in the major leagues. You're throwing yourself into a heated competition and squaring off against tens of thousands of other writers who also have the same lofty dream: to see their books on the Internet and between the bookshelves. Many of these writers, your competitors, have published previous books or have strong writing and publishing backgrounds; they may have great contacts, know the ropes, and know what it takes to succeed. They could be marketing juggernauts and be familiar with how to write a bestseller.

So, if you want to play in the same arena, you must:

- Understand the rules and how to play the game
- Learn how writing and publishing work, what they entail, and how the industry functions
- Find out what is expected of you
- Learn what you must do to succeed

These lessons are not too hard to learn, and once you understand them, you will find yourself better equipped to enter the highly specialized world of publishing and to boost your chances of authoring a published book.

With the advent of The Internet and the influx and enormous growth of self-publishers and hybrid houses like Morgan-James, founded by David Hancock, many entrepreneurs with a unique idea and a strong and well-developed platform can submit their proposals and obtain the exciting opportunity to become a published author. In fact, there is an unbelievable breadth of fantastic resources and educational programs out there to help potential authors learn the essential guidelines and principles to create high quality books. One of these is Author101Online.com, a newly developed and unique website that focuses on offering insightful and exciting information for prospective authors. This website offers visitors strategic and detailed resources on book marketing and publishing. They are so dedicated to helping authors that any visitor to the site receives three free training sessions on book marketing provided by some of the most reputable and noted experts in the field. But to become a *successful* author is an entirely different story and challenge.

So before we get into the specifics of how to write nonfiction books, we would like to briefly walk you through the writing and publishing processes. We would like to touch upon what's involved and how it basically works. Our purpose is to give you an overview that will lay the proper foundation for the information that lies ahead, to give you context to more readily understand the material we will address later in this book.

Rick Says

So why write a book? Do it because you want to teach someone, help someone, and make a difference. Write a book out of love. Don't write a book because you just want to make money. The odds are a book won't make you rich, but the satisfaction in your accomplishment will be priceless. Your book can change people's lives. Write it from your heart and then maybe, just maybe, tons of money will follow.

The Elements of Writing

When many aspiring writers decide to author a nonfiction book, they have no idea what they're getting into. They have little realization or understanding of what they will have to do. Remember, writing the book is just part of the process to become a successful author. All they know is that they want to write a book, so they dive right in, but unfortunately, they don't really know how to proceed. They begin playing the game without understanding the rules. They may not know where to start, and if they do, they may not know where to go from there.

Writing a book is a major undertaking; it's a long and often difficult process that many would-be authors start, but fail to complete. Completing a book takes knowledge, work, discipline, and determination. And it takes lots of planning.

Robyn Says

You can write and publish a wonderful, successful book; it's completely within your grasp. And to help you get there, Rick and I are here to show you the ropes. Rick and I are experts with those ropes; between us we have written and published scores of books and we've helped innumerable aspiring authors—just like you— to get their books written and in print. Of course, there are never any guarantees in the book business. So if you give up too quickly, or after you get a stack of rejections, you're bound to miss out on reaching the goal of becoming an author. www.robynspizman.com

While I have written many books including *When Words Matter Most* and *The Thank You Book*, as well as books on gift-giving, parenting, philanthropy and books on careers and work with Tory Johnson and inspirational books with H. Jackson Brown, Jr., I have learned so much about the world of books. It took years of writing to hit the New York Times Bestseller's list, but I have enjoyed every minute of writing. I have also loved lecturing on book writing and encouraging other writers and non-writers alike to write the book that's inside their hearts.

When I wrote *When Words Matter Most*, I discovered and shared the most profound words, actions and deeds to let someone know how much you appreciate and cherish them. This book continues to make a difference and serves as a meaningful book to gift to yourself or anyone for any occasion. When I'm asked what is the best part of being an author? That's easy to answer. It is simply gratifying to know that a book I have written can brighten the world and leave a legacy of caring and kindness.

We know that you can do it, we want to see you do it, and we're happy to help. If at times the road seems bumpy, don't become discouraged or give up. Keep at it and stay with it—the best-seller list awaits you!

While all writers approach the process differently, the following steps are usually involved in creating a nonfiction book. Although we could break down this process in far greater detail, we have decided to limit it to the following four items for this overview. For now, our objective is just to tell you what is involved and later we will describe these items more fully. The general steps in writing a book are:

Finding the Idea

All books begin with a basic idea or concept, with determining what the book will be about. A successful book must offer readers some benefit. It must tell them how to solve a problem, complete a task, learn or read about an interesting individual. Since all ideas don't make good, salable books, writers must come up with ideas that they can develop to hold readers' interest for the length of an entire book. They must test their ideas to see if they have enough substance for a book. When agents and editors hear about book ideas, they frequently comment that the idea would make a good magazine article but is not enough for a book. Remember that most publishers and editors receive thousands of book proposals and manuscripts each and every month. To stand out, you have to clearly outline your concept, and then demonstrate how you will package it in an exceptional and marketable manner.

Conducting Research

Writers conduct research to learn about and gather more information on the subjects of their books. Before they begin book projects, many writers have stores of research materials already on hand, especially those who write about their businesses or their areas of expertise. When writers conduct research, they may be looking for background information from books and articles. They can also conduct interviews and surveys; review case studies; take classes, lessons, and workshops; make site visits; or undertake activities or experiences to better understand what is involved.

Erase those grim memories of the research you were forced to conduct for school. Researching a book you're writing can be completely different. First, you're looking into subjects that interest you, not boring stuff that you were assigned. Second, you're researching for yourself, to obtain information, not because it's part of a mandatory school project. Finally, research can be fun; it can fill in questions and bring you greater understanding, and you can interview, meet, speak with, and get to know marvelous, intelligent, and interesting people. But also remember part of your responsibility in the initial research is studying the market and your competition. Consider market appeal and whether or not you are fishing in a genre with lots of fish, or none of them at all.

Organizing Information

Keeping track of research materials and organizing them makes projects more efficient and orderly. Since voluminous information can be involved in the writing of a book, many writers need to quickly access all of it, which becomes far easier when that information is housed in specific locations and is well organized. Some writers develop intricate systems for filing and organizing their data. How information is maintained and organized can also be critical because many writers create outlines for their books and chapters directly from their research material, and others write straight from the information in their files.

Writing the Book

The actual process of putting information on a page consists primarily of two stages—composing and editing—that often overlap. Most writers start to write by referring to their outlines, explaining the points they've listed, and expanding on them. This is the composing phase, and as they compose sentences, paragraphs, and sections, most writers constantly edit and revise. Some don't initially edit, but concentrate on getting information down. Then, when they've got it on paper, they come back and revise. Most writers also edit after they've completed drafts. Some edit a lot, even obsessively. In fact, it is not entirely uncommon for authors to hire expert book architects like Justin Spizman (www.justinspizman.com) to develop and edit the entire book at the conclusion of the writing process. Remember, sometimes you can't see the forest for the trees. This is your baby and since you have been intimately working on your book for lengthy periods of time, another set of eyes on your book can often be extremely helpful. It is not considered cheating or cutting corners. You have still done the heavy lifting. Rather, it is an opportunity to fine-tune and turn a good book into a great one.

A fifth element that is essential to the book-writing process is promotion. In addition to the steps listed above, writers must enthusiastically promote their books; it's vital to their success. While promotion is an equal partner in the success of a book, we will not be discussing it at length in this book because we've written about it extensively in an earlier book.

However, as a result of my over 35 years of book writing and decades of serving as a communication's expert, I continue to consult with authors and companies on how to promote yourself, discover your big idea and write the book you were born to author. I also run a PR firm that specializes in consulting with authors about their books and public relation's campaigns. Every book is a gift and an opportunity to make a difference! www.robynspizman.com

The Elements of Publishing

In addition to writing their books, most writers want to get them published by traditional publishing houses. So, in order to sell their books to traditional publishers, they usually must go through a number of specific steps. As an alternative to traditional publishing, they can self-publish or publish e-books, which we are not going to address at this time. Instead, we're going to concentrate on the traditional publishing process, how it works, and the elements involved. Although the process may differ from publisher to publisher, most houses operate along similar, general lines.

Do your homework; learn which publishing houses specialize in nonfiction books in your subject area. Even though your top choice may be overloaded with books on your topic and may not be buying, it is still a good idea for you to know the nonfiction publishers who could do a great job for you. Sometimes it is all about timing and a specific need. A house may not be accepting new books in your category, but if you made a positive initial impression, then you will be at the front of their mind when the need is there.

Submissions to publishing companies are generally made two ways: through literary agents and directly by writers to editors at the houses. According to estimates, roughly 80 percent of the books that are traditionally published are received from agents. Many publishing companies prefer agented submissions, and many won't accept unagented works.

The traditional publishing process generally proceeds as follows:

A Query

To start the process, writers or their agents usually send query letters or e-mails to publishers, asking whether they would be interested in publishing the proposed books. Queries describe the projects and the authors and try to generate enough interest for the editor to request a book proposal. An agent's connections and relationships are extraordinarily valuable during this time. Thus, make sure you interview your agent and consider his or her qualifications as well as the houses that he or she has worked with in the past before making a selection. When shopping a new project, finding the right fit is crucial to the overall success of the book.

Editor Review

Editors read the queries. If they are interested, they usually ask the agents or writers to submit a book proposal. Editors will also inform writers if they are not interested, or they may request additional information. When they receive the information they requested, they may ask the writer to submit a proposal, or they may say no.

Book Proposal

Editors want book proposals that follow a particular format, which is usually specified on the publisher's website. Make sure you do your research. It is possible a publisher may reject your proposal simply because you did not follow their preferred format. Generally, they want an opening description of the book or an overview that explains, in two or three pages, the book's concept, the problems it will solve, and the benefits it will provide. The proposal should include the author's biography, describe the markets for the book, explain the author's promotion plan, and analyze comparable books. It should also give the book's table of contents, chapter summaries, and a sample chapter or chapters.

Proposal Review

When editors receive book proposals, they, or their assistants, read them. Other editors, as well as marketing and other personnel, may also read proposals. When readers like a proposal and think that it has merit, they will write a report, attach it to the proposal, and send it to their superiors or the house's acquisition committee or board.

Committee/Board Review

Although the precise process at each house varies, proposals usually undergo committee reviews. If the editor is initially interested, he or she will turn over the book to his review committee for further feedback and scrutiny. Some firms have several committee reviews, while others have just one. Members of the publisher's editorial board, marketing staff, and other personnel usually participate in meetings. An editor generally champions the proposal while the others ask questions and give opinions and provide information about similar or competitive books. Proposals are picked apart and challenged to make sure that they are good candidates for publication and fit with the publishing house's current line. Discussions are held on whether the company should commit more time and resources to the book.

Market Analysis

Since publishing houses are commercial enterprises, acquisition decisions are market driven. At every stage of the process, editors, committee members, and other company personnel will examine whether they think the book can make money. Salespeople and executives may seek the opinions of large retail booksellers. A book will seldom get the green light unless all involved believe that it will turn a profit.

Acquisition Decision

Who makes the final purchasing decision can also vary. Depending on the specific house, acquisition decisions are made by editors in chief, chief operating officers, or executive committees such as editorial boards. The groups charged with giving final approval can range in size from ten to thirty people. The decision makers determine how much they are willing to pay for the book and then the publisher sends a publishing contract to the writer or his or her agent.

Negotiations

When contracts are sent, the parties then negotiate the terms with the author's literary agent, or directly with the author if he or she is not represented by an agent. When terms are agreed upon, the contract is revised to reflect the changes, and each party signs. The author's first advance against royalty payment is then usually paid.

The Writing

An editor is assigned to the book, and that editor usually contacts the writer to discuss the plan for writing the book. Editors frequently explain their concerns and inform authors about their expectations. They discuss how they want to see the book progress and when materials should be submitted.

Postsubmission

When the manuscript is completed, it's forwarded to the publisher, and the editor reads it. Editors make suggestions that they feel will help the book. Writers then revise the manuscript in accordance with the editor's comments and resubmit it.

If the revisions make the manuscript acceptable, a portion of the advance against royalties is often payable.

Production

Books that are produced in-house are then copyedited, designed, formatted, and indexed. Frequently, some or all of these tasks are outsourced. After manuscripts are copyedited, they are sent to authors to address the copyeditor's query marks. The authors answer the queries and accept or reject the copyeditor's changes and return the manuscript. In the production process, designs are developed for both the book's cover and interior content. The publishers usually make all design decisions; they may show authors designs in progress, but they generally retain the final say. That's not to say authors don't ever have a voice. So, when you have an opinion, it's best to give it early on before cover designs are completed.

Promotion

The promotional campaign for a book is usually developed by the publisher's sales and publicity departments in consultation with the book editor. In recent years, publishing houses have shifted the bulk of the promotion responsibility from themselves to their authors. In fact, most publishers expect authors to diligently work to create a strong platform, social media presence, and marketing campaign. The resources are simply not as they once were. Publishing houses can only offer so much support to new authors and projects. As we will discuss later in this chapter, they expect authors to be their "promotion partners." So, authors, at their own expense, frequently hire book publicists like us to work with their publisher's publicity departments.

"Publishing houses are looking for authors who are salespeople," observes Louis Patler, coauthor of *If It Ain't Broke, Break It* (Warner Business Books, 1992). So, it's important to know that the publisher has a marketing plan to sell the book. Therefore, Patler and his agent spend a lot of time during negotiations making sure that the prospective publisher has a general perspective on how it will handle the marketing for his book. He believes that the publisher's promotion plan is a major negotiating consideration in a book deal.

My Favorite Part

T. Harv Eker, author of *Secrets of the Millionaire Mind* (Collins, 2005), jokes that his favorite part of the writing process "is finishing." He loves to come up with "stuff that is really hot and feeling, 'Wow, this is really good.'" Or writing something so funny that it makes him laugh out loud. Eker loves being really creative and the spontaneity of good ides, good examples, good stories, and a well-written statement "that comes out through you. Something that is wise, profound, and a higher wisdom."

Publishing Is a Business

Now that you understand some of what writing and publishing entail, it's essential that you be aware of a few additional concepts. The first is that publishing is a business. Never forget that publishing companies are profit-making enterprises that exist in order to make money, because it will affect your, and your publisher's, decisions. If they are unsure of whether or not they can turn profit on your book, they will ultimately pass on the project.

When writers get involved in publishing, they often enter at a serious disadvantage. First, they're outsiders who can easily be swallowed up by a mysterious, complex, and often baffling industry. When they enter the publishing world, the playing field isn't level. Like Las Vegas, publishing is stacked in favor of the houses. The publishers exercise the power and control, and they play by their rules—and those rules exist to ensure that the publishers make money.

Writers often encounter problems because of their naiveté. They attach romantic notions and lofty ideals to publishers; they think that the industry exists to advance the art of literature and culture and believe that they're a part of a noble pursuit. Writers are often blinded by their need to become published authors, so they're willing to swallow whatever it takes. They often fail to realize that publishing is a business; its primary objective is to make money. Virtually all publishing decisions are based on the bottom line, not the love of the game.

A small number of international companies control some 80 percent of the publishing industry. They are constantly acquiring and growing. These companies are businesses that deal in the commodity of books. Although they may have high artistic standards, they are not charities or benevolent associations. They are not cultural foundations that exist solely to serve writers and the public good; they are businesses that exist to make money.

For writers, this understanding is critical because it can impact whether they can get their books published and make them successful. The need for books to make money is a reality, and if writers hope to succeed, they must shape their books in ways that will promote publishing companies' needs.

The Platform Requirement

One of the most significant changes in publishing in the past decade has been the shifting by publishers of the responsibility for promoting authors' books from themselves to the authors. In the past, publishing houses actively publicized their authors' books. They operated large, active, in-house publicity departments that were fully engaged in promoting the titles on their lists. Most notable authors were sent on extensive, nationwide book tours, for which the houses picked up the tab. Now, with the exception of the biggest, best-selling, and celebrity authors, those tours are a memory, and whatever tours are booked are far less extensive than those of the past.

Attorney and Strategic Advisor, Peter Hoppenfeld, discusses the power of the platform. He says, "Authors today, more so than ever, must be sharing their ideas on multiple platforms (website, blog, video, Facebook, LinkedIn, Twitter, Pinterest, etc...) and should be actively and proactively involved in building an audience or community. What works for some may not work for all. It is important to find your 'magic sauce;' the mix of message and audience that builds your brand and gets your book and your message to your ideal community."

Somewhere along the line, publishers made the unilateral decision to shift the publicity burden from themselves to their authors. Now, they consider authors their "promotional partners," which means that the authors are expected to do most of the work and fund much of the publicity. Authors are expected to vigorously promote their books and to do so at their own expense. In-house publicity departments have been pared to the bone and are now manned by a few overworked publicists who constantly struggle to keep up with their responsibilities.

In addition, publishers have erected a substantial new barrier that has made it difficult for many writers to get their nonfiction books published. Publishers call it the platform requirement, which essentially means that publishers want authors who have continuing national visibility and an established following. In short, publishers generally won't publish business, psychology, parenting, relationship, and other books for authors who don't have national platforms. They require authors to create and maintain strong social media connections and presence.

Today, publishers want authors who can sell their books because they make frequent speaking engagements; regularly write articles or columns; and have strong media and Internet presences, large mailing lists, government posts, faculty positions, or professional affiliations. To further narrow the field, many publishers have extended the platform requirement to previously published writers.

"The bar for platforms has been raised to almost absurd heights," Encino, California, agent Sharlene Martin, of Martin Literary Management, explains.

"A whole plethora of good writing is being ignored because it doesn't have the promotional hooks that publishers are now demanding."

When writers who don't have platforms come to Martin, she tells them "they're not ready; that they're before their time." She explains that writing a great book is just a part of the package and that they have to build their platform.

Agent Richard Curtis offers some encouragement. "The bar in publishing has been raised extremely high, but not impossibly high," he says. "A good book will still rise to the surface if it's a really good book."

It's important to impress on publishers that you're willing to vigorously promote your book. Work to build your platform. Start blogging, building social media presence, and taking any and every opportunity to present as an expert on your proposed topic.

Self-Publishing

When most people talk about publishing, they are generally referring to traditional publishing, the process in which an established publishing house buys an author's book and takes all the steps necessary to bring it to market. That may include editing the completed manuscript; designing the book and its cover; and printing, distributing, and promoting it.

Rick Says

Self-publishing is now a realistic alternative for many nonfiction writers, and experts expect it to become more so in the coming years. Self-publishing allows authors to publish books that they could not sell through traditional publishing channels. And by self-publishing, writers can keep more of the money their books earn and their intellectual property. Self-published authors can also avoid many of the necessities of traditional publishing, like writing query letters and book proposals, which many writers hate. And they don't have to hire and share their royalties with literary agents.

On the other hand, self-publishing can involve an enormous amount of work, and the learning curve can be steep. Self-published authors must learn how to, or hire others to, perform the many tasks that traditional houses perform. In addition to writing their books, they must assume responsibility for editing, designing, printing, distributing, and promoting them, which can be time consuming, stressful, and expensive. Fortunately for them, a number of businesses have now cropped up that specialize in servicing self-publisher's needs. Some may offer just one service, while others may offer a turnkey approach to publishing your book. Regardless, these specialized service providers are available and can do a great job at helping you produce a top-notch and professional book.

Instead of getting a chunk of royalty money up front, self-publishers have to pay a steady stream of costs before they receive any income. Selling self-published books can be iffy because many booksellers won't stock them or will handle only a few of the more successful ones. Thus, distribution and shelf life can often feel like an uphill battle.

Since self-publishing has become more popular, traditional publishers have bought books that were originally self-published, or they have agreed to publish self-published authors' subsequent works. So, self-publishing can be a launching pad for authors who otherwise could not get their books published.

Finally, self-published books can be effective in advancing authors' careers. They can be viewed as unbelievable calling cards. While they may not carry the prestige of titles published by distinguished houses, self-published books look good on authors' resumes; when they're held up or projected during personal appearances; and when signed copies of them are given to influential colleagues, contacts, and friends. During personal appearances, self-published books can also sell well from the back of the room.

My Least Favorite Part

For Stedman Graham, author of *Diversity: Leaders Not Labels* (Simon & Schuster, June 2006), the least favorite part of writing a book is the fact that it takes so long. He figures that it takes a full five years from the time he comes up with an idea until it hits the bookshelves. "You need the patience to stay on it and sustain your energy for the duration of the project—and that's why you must be passionate about it," Graham adds.

MEET JOEY REIMAN

Joey Reiman never gave up. He is the brilliant author who gave a thumbs up to his readers, the literary world and wrote a can't-miss book about creating a purposeful life. Now, an International Speaker, Founder and CEO of the first global ideation company BrightHouse, Joey's newest book *THUMBS UP!: Five Steps to Create The Life You Dreamed Of* (BenBella Books), Spring 2015, is a book written for anyone who has a dream or an idea and needs a dose of focus and a tank of fuel for life. Staying positive and optimistic about the journey of becoming an author is essential. Reiman nails that in his book. Grab a cup of this Joe-y at www.dailyjoey.com and visit www.joeyreiman.com to learn about how he became an author extraordinaire. We give Reiman a thumbs up for never giving up. His best advice, "Don't follow the money. Look for the meaning. When you find it, the money will follow."

Action Items

1. List the four elements of writing.
2. Outline the elements usually involved in the traditional publishing process.
3. How many companies control what percentage of all book sales?
4. Explain what the platform requirement is.
5. List three items that could make self-publishing advantageous to authors.

·················· **REMEMBER** ··················

Writing and getting a nonfiction book published is an enormous and extremely satisfying achievement. However, to successfully do so, you need to understand what is entailed. To write a book, you have to come up with an idea, research it, organize all of your information, and then write the text and edit it. Then, you must actively promote the book.

Traditional publishing entails a number of steps that aspiring writers must understand and be prepared to complete. They must realize that publishing is a business, so the books they pitch must have commercial potential, or traditional publishers will probably pass on them. To increase the odds that their books will be successful, publishers now want writers who have national platforms and followings.

Chapter 2

GETTING STARTED

*My aim is to put down on paper what I see and what I feel
in the best and simplest way.*
—Ernest Hemingway

This chapter covers:
- Start writing
- Expectations
- Read, read, read
- Create a plan
- Work in progress
- Understand your goals
- Passion and perseverance

For many writers, the hardest part of writing a book is getting started. Think about your own experience. When you tried to write your book, did you go through times when you sat there like a boulder, staring blankly at the screen or the paper while nothing came out except buckets of sweat? Did all of your ideas, those brilliant thoughts that had been bouncing around your mind forever, suddenly vanish and dry up the moment you tried to write? Was the experience belittling? Were you discouraged? Did it make you feel like a failure or a dunce?

Did you get a paragraph or two down, then reread what you had written, only to find that what you composed was total garbage that even you couldn't understand? Did it make you so disappointed that you told yourself that you're just not a writer? Did it cause you to quit and never want to write again?

Well, obviously not completely if you're reading this book. Even if you just picked up this title as a curiosity, as a last resort, or on a whim, something inside you, probably very deep down inside you, still has hope and wants to write. It may be just a tiny spark or minuscule flicker, but it's still alive and not dead. Go with it; don't ignore it, because it needs to be explored, examined, nourished, nurtured, and given a chance.

For those of you who have not started, you may need a roadmap and some fuel. If so, you've also come to the right place.

In the pages that follow, we're going to help you rekindle that flame and build it into a blazing conflagration. We're going to show you how to get started and write. Inexperienced writers often struggle because they don't know how to proceed, or they give up because approaches that they've been told to follow just don't work for them.

Robyn Says

So you've decided to write a nonfiction book. Congratulations! I've spent over three decades writing nonfiction; in fact, it's how I got started. I find nonfiction a rewarding way to help people and share my knowledge. And I also learn so much along the way.

When I teach groups on how to start writing books, I suggest that they first write a Dear Reader letter, which is a promise they make in writing to their readers. In the letter, first explain why you are the perfect person to write this book. Then include what readers will gain from reading it and what you promise to deliver. Then reread your letter. If the benefits are clear, then it's time to start writing your book. If not, regroup and refocus. But look at it like a contract between you and your audience. Keep the promises you make. By the way, your Dear Reader letter can be incorporated into your book's introduction or used to jump-start your writing.

Start Writing

Get in the habit of writing; begin practicing your craft and decide that you're going to work on it steadily. If writing is truly important to you, set aside a specific time each day to actually put pen to paper. Even if you can spare only ten or fifteen minutes, set aside that time to write.

At the very least, write a page a day. Before you know it, the book will take off. Writing is like starting a diet. Once you get a few days under your belt, you feel better and it's easier to continue.

New York Times Best-Selling Author Cory Doctorow offers his prescription for writing a book: "Write every day. Anything you do every day gets easier. If you're insanely busy, make the amount that you write every day small, but do it every day. Write even when the mood isn't right. You can't tell if what you're writing is good or bad while you're writing it. Write when the book sucks and it isn't going anywhere. Just keep writing. It doesn't suck. Your conscious is having a panic attack because it doesn't believe your subconscious knows what it's doing. Write even when the world is chaotic. You don't need a cigarette, silence, music, a comfortable chair, or inner peace to write. You just need ten minutes and a writing implement."

When Robyn began writing, her children were young, so she had to write when they were napping or between their activities. Frequently, she would even write during the middle of the night. Often, you have to grab whatever writing time is available. It takes time, effort, determination, and sometimes, even sleepless nights.

Tell your family and friends that you will be writing each morning between 7:30 and 9:00. Ask them not to phone you or disturb you. Turn off your cellphone so you don't hear it chime in. Then every day, at the appointed time, sit down and write.

Create a support system. Explain your goals to your friends and family so they can fully support you and hold you accountable. Clear off your calendar and desk to give yourself the physical, mental, and emotional space to write. Stay highly organized so you can manage everything in your life and still have time to write.

If you have book ideas, wonderful, start working to develop them now. If not, write whatever comes into your mind. Write about your thoughts, feelings, experiences, and knowledge. Write about people, things, and places you know. Write about what you would like to learn. Ask yourself questions and then answer them, even if your answers make no sense.

As you write, place more importance on the fact that you're writing than on the quality of what you compose. There is always time to clean it up later. Place a greater premium on the act of writing than on what you pen. If you want to be a writer, you must actually write. So get started, practice, and learn. Keep at it because after a while, it will produce good results.

Increase your book radar. Write down book ideas and titles as they enter your mind. Then keep them on an ongoing list. Since ideas and titles often arrive at the strangest times, write them down immediately because they can vanish as quickly as they come. And trying to recall forgotten ideas can drive you nuts.

Expectations

Don't let your expectations, including any fears of failing or succeeding, stop you. Identify what you expect from yourself and from your writing and whether those expectations are realistic.

One of the difficulties with writing is that most of us speak effortlessly, and we do so all the time. Since we usually have little trouble verbally expressing ourselves, we expect that we should be able to be just as clear the moment we try to write. But let's take a look at whether that expectation is realistic—even for those of us who did some writing in school and subsequently in our jobs, in letters and via e-mail.

The truth is that most of us speak constantly, but we write infrequently. It can be a difficult task to take the thoughts in your head and bring them to life on paper. Even the most prolific writers don't write nearly as often as they speak.

And many of us hardly write at all. Speaking comes easily and naturally. We've had a lot of practice. When we're in contact with others, we usually respond reflexively by just opening our mouths and letting the words and thoughts pour out. And what we say is usually easily understood.

Writing, however, doesn't flow so naturally or fluidly. It is a learned trade. We may have to think about each word, sentence, and transition. We may have to spell words in our minds and plan their sequence. Writing is also governed by many strange, complex, and long-forgotten rules that we memorized in school. So when we write, we may struggle with grammar, structure, spelling, and making ourselves clear.

To compound the problem, writing has permanence. Unlike spoken words, which evaporate and fade over time, written words hang around. You never know who might find them, comment on them, quote them, or even use them against you. While our oral utterances can be forgotten or denied, our writing is self-documenting and can live to haunt us forever. Our writing can be indelible.

When we speak, informality and lack of precision are usually accepted and frequently encouraged. We don't feel that each word is being scrutinized or being judged. But when we write, formality reigns: we are expected to be clear, correct, and exact, and we feel like we're being graded.

So, for a variety of reasons, writing is difficult, even painful, for many. Expecting that you will write well the first few go-rounds is usually unrealistic. It can take a lifetime of writing before you hit your stride. Even the most accomplished authors have numerous rewrites—especially the most accomplished authors. Countless writers, highly successful professionals, stressed to us how hard it is for them to write. Judy Ford, author of over fifteen books that have sold over seven hundred thousand copies, tells us, "I sit at the computer and give birth to a barbed-wire fence. You have to sit there even though it's very painful and the labor is very long." But through that pain, Ford loves to write and continues to turn out wonderful books.

Writers' expectations of themselves can place them under undue pressure and make their tasks infinitely harder. Instead of beating themselves up and focusing on results, they must approach writing as a process that involves trial, error, time, understanding, and growth.

Rick Says

Look at it this way. If you were an inexperienced woodworker, you wouldn't expect to build a fine custom cabinet on your initial attempt or even after the first few tries. Most folks would start with a simpler assignment, gain skill and experience, and work their way up. They would understand that they have to learn to master their craft, how to handle their materials and develop a touch. They would be patient and understanding—and so should you.

Writing is a fine craft that takes time to master. Sure, some writers are blessed with special talent that makes writing easier for them, but they're in the vast minority. Most of us have to labor; we must write, edit, and rewrite and then do it over and over again. Some may even have to bring in professionals to help perfect their trade. But there is no shame in that. So let yourself go through the process; understand that it will take time; and allow yourself to make mistakes, to learn from them and grow. That's how you find your voice.

Read, Read, Read

Reading is the best foundation for writing. If you don't read frequently, start now. Begin with newspapers and magazines and work your way up. Take the time to surf the Internet for an hour in the morning or evening and read articles from various websites. This may help you to acknowledge and familiarize yourself with different styles, tones, and voices. It will help you to identify your preferences and formulate your own voice.

Reading exposes you to writers who excel at expressing the written word. It teaches you to recognize good writing, including your own, and shows you what and whom to emulate. It helps you develop standards and determine what to write, how to write, and what to avoid. Recognizing what doesn't work for you is just as valuable as understanding what does.

Katherine Ramsland, author of over twenty-five books, including *The Human Predator: A Historical Chronicle of Serial Murder and Forensic Investigation* (Berkeley Hardcover, 2005), advises, "Read, read, read, but only read what is well written and don't waste your time reading junk. Body memories are important to the writing process and if you read junk, it's often what you will write.

However, if you read quality, that's what you will try to produce. Readers form a psychological sense of rhythm, pace, language and depth of meaning through reading. It sinks in and becomes a part of them. Don't expect to be a writer if you're not a reader."

Reading introduces writers to other authors' "flow," the psychological sense that Ramsland described. Flow gives life to writers' words and becomes their voice. It has an intoxicating effect that writers crave.

Reading also gives writers a steady source of information, and information breeds ideas, which is an essential piece for any writer. Writers we interviewed for this book stressed how many different publications they read in order to get new ideas and information, and how these publications inspire them and fill up their "information banks." A number reported that they read five to seven newspapers each day, several on weekends, and that they constantly devour magazines. Award-Winning Author and Book Architect Justin Spizman (www.justinspizman.com) told us, "I spend just as much time reading as I do writing. When working with my clients, I find that evaluating and understanding their writing styles offers the exciting opportunity to identify and transcend their voice, which makes for a better end result. To me, reading the work of talented writers is an integral part of the writing process."

Many writers disclosed that they make it a point to read about subjects other than their areas of expertise because it informs them about methods and concepts they can import into their own fields. This cross-fertilization strengthens their writing and injects it with additional creativity that was spurred by their reading.

Reading also increases writers' curiosity. In most cases, the more they learn about various subjects, the more they want to know. Time and time again, writers tell us that the simple act of reading another writer's book inspired a book of their own. Their curiosity can cause them to question or challenge accepted notions in their particular field that may no longer apply or were never really true.

My Favorite Part

For Mary Roach, the best part of the writing process is writing certain material that she knows will be "a hell of a lot of fun to write"—passages where she has good material and it comes out easily. "The fact that you feel good about it makes you relax more and the writing becomes more enjoyable. Those days are great when you're working with material where you can't go wrong."

Create a Plan

Many would-be writers start their books impulsively and haphazardly, which seldom works. When they get good ideas and inspirations, they rush to get them down. Frequently, they don't think about how they should proceed and just feel that the strength of their ideas, inspiration, and passion will carry them through—and sometimes, they're right. However, in most cases, they're charting a course for failure. Great writing takes detailed preparation.

Many aspiring writers also go through what authors call "brain dumps," in which they unload whatever ideas or information are on their minds. While brain dumps can be good starting points and can help in identifying valuable material, they can also create real messes because torrents of ideas, information, and emotions are released without sequence, order, or design. Brain dumps can produce floods of loosely connected concepts that are not thoroughly thought through or researched. So when writers subsequently read their ramblings, they become discouraged and toss everything out—the good as well as the bad. Often times, we suggest working with a collaborator or writer to help navigate this otherwise insurmountable information. Sometimes, another set of eyes can truly be the difference between a good book and a great one.

Writing a book may start with a flash of inspiration, but then it takes planning, organization, and work, work, work. It's a long, involved progression—like running a marathon, producing a movie, or conducting a complex campaign. It takes discipline, dedication, and effort. It won't happen overnight, but if you stay the course, it can eventually come to life. If you try to do it all at once, it can overwhelm you. So it must be planned. And when it is, when you create a structure, writing a book can become fun and fulfilling and can do wonders for your ego and your career.

Never think of a book as a one-time venture; always consider it as part of a larger plan. Whether you want to build a career as a writer, or write to build your business or another aspect of your life, focus on creating a supportive following. As Seth Godin, best-selling author of *Purple Cow* (Portfolio, 2003), says, "Nonfiction is almost never about the writing. It's about your following, the permission asset you have with readers, the boost you can get in starting conversations. A publisher will not make you succeed. Those days are long, long gone." Plan for the long run, beyond any single book.

We will discuss planning in greater detail in Chapter 5, "Planning and Outlining."

Work in Progress

The process of developing and writing a book is always a work in progress that is subject to change. The book that you originally conceive may end up as something totally different. As Lillian Hellman said, "Nothing you write, if you hope to be good, will ever come out as you first hoped."

"A book is organic and constantly changes form," Jeff Greenwald, author of *Scratching the Surface: Impressions of Planet Earth from Hollywood to Shiraz* (Regent Press, 2002), notes. "It grows very gradually as it's being written and things are always being shifted and changed. You always have to be open to the evolution that a process goes through."

No matter how fixed they may seem, every element of a book can, and often will, change. The very ideas and themes that inspired the book and seemed solid as bedrock may be missing from the published version. While you are writing your book, you may find that key ideas are flawed or the latest techniques are impractical, or revolutionary new innovations could take hold. Great leads could go nowhere, and major interview subjects could have absolutely nothing interesting to say.

So you have to be flexible and willing to adapt, quickly change, and put in any extra work needed. Keep your focus, and constantly remember that it's more important for your book to be strong, accurate, and up to date than it is to cling stubbornly to old ideas and information that may be wrong or outdated. For that reason, this is the second version of this book. We spent countless hours updating the material to ensure it was relevant, accurate, and helpful to potential authors at all levels.

Understand Your Goals

To write a nonfiction book, it's crucial to set achievable goals and create workable plans to achieve them. Unless you're into experimentation or just want to meander along for the ride, you need a road map; you need to know where you're going. You must be clear about your objective, and what you want to achieve. So, the first step is to clarify your goals.

Understanding your goals can be elusive for they too can change. The first goals that pop into writers' minds are often not what they truly want. Or they mature and develop and their goals and values change. Recognize that there is nothing wrong with that. It is just part of the process.

The best way to determine your actual goals is to ask yourself nonjudgmentally why you want to write a book. Be honest. Dig deep to find the actual reasons why you want to write your book, because they can influence the choices you make and the direction you chart. Do you have a point to make, a story to tell, or a feat to accomplish? Admit if you want fame, fortune, and recognition, but understand that they may be difficult to attain.

Before you begin to write, after you are clear on why you want to write, create a step-by-step plan. Think about the best way to get information and understand your topic, how you can find out what you should read and whom you should interview. Assess the competition, learn how you differ, and identify your niche. Consider those people you'd like to include in your book and begin to sculpt a plan to connect with them.

Set financially realistic goals, which means not expecting to make a fortune from your book. In fact, don't write a book to make money, because you will probably be deeply disappointed. As Louis Patler points out, even books that sell well may make questionable financial sense.

"If you get a 10 percent royalty on a book with a $20.00 cover price," Patler notes, "you will get somewhere between 80 cents to a dollar on each book sold after everything is deducted: discounts, agents' commissions and amounts retained. So, if you get a $10,000 advance, it takes a lot of book sales to earn that back. People don't understand that a *New York Times* bestseller will sell approximately 50,000 copies in a six-month period and you know how few books sell that well. So, if you do the math, on a 50,000-copy seller, the maximum you're going to earn before taxes is $50,000, which may not be much of a return considering all the time, effort, and expenses you put in."

In addition to not making you rich, you're also unlikely to receive widespread fame. However, your book can produce other rewards that can be equally or more beneficial. It can help you build your business and career; make outstanding contacts; bring you and your family enormous pride and satisfaction; build a strong personal or professional platform; and help you create a wonderful, rewarding life.

Your writing can also help you build other income streams. For instance, it can bring you new clients and customers who hire you as a consultant, advisor, or trainer for their staffs. A book can be a fantastic calling card that generates business and paints you as a formidable expert in your area of business. Nonfiction authors also make popular public speakers, and your book could help you launch a lucrative speaking career. Accomplished speakers tell us that they earn as much in two or three speeches as they do from all the royalties they are paid during any one book's life. Books can also bring other and more engaging writing assignments. We see these success stories all of the time. In fact, Book Architect Justin Spizman (www.justinspizman.com) told us, "I once worked with a very successful sports agent to write a self-help book. When we started our book together, she was working seventy-hour weeks. With her hard work, intelligent positioning, and her new book, she shifted her focus on speaking and began charging premium fees to present to large companies while working less and spending more time with her family."

Despite the lack of financial rewards, most nonfiction authors love being writers and would not change. "Writing books is the single defining thing that has happened in my career," Brad Schoenfeld, author of *Look Great Naked* (Penguin, 2001) and five other books, remarks. "Although I've done well monetarily from my books, you won't get 'rich rich.' The real rewards come from everything else that comes from writing a book."

Schoenfeld's books have brought him greater stature in his field and have strengthened his credibility with clients. They have also given him "entree into all sorts of other areas; people hear about you, endorsement deals come your way, videos are made and doors open," he explains.

My Least Favorite Part

For Jeff Greenwald, the least enjoyable parts of authoring books are the business aspects, dealing with publicity and legal issues and arranging interviews and their logistics. Greenwald doesn't like selling his books and wishes that he could just write them and not have to pitch and sell them. He is uncomfortable with marketing departments, even though he knows that they really determine whether a book will be published or not. A lot of other writers have a very keen sense of what will sell, which Greenwald has never had.

Passion and Perseverance

To write a successful book, you must be passionate about both your subject and your book. You must breathe, eat, sleep, and live with them. You have to know your subject inside out and make sure that you don't lose interest in it. Many aspiring authors get excited about their subjects and go through a quick, torrid romance; then they lose interest and the project dies. Think about the size of the graveyard where those books that were never finished go to rest in peace. We are comfortable in saying that less than ten percent of books that are started are actually finished. It is a long road ahead, but one that is enormously rewarding.

To keep the fire flaming, you must believe in your book and in the benefits it will give others. You can make a difference. Your book is simply the megaphone to voice your message. When you truly believe, the hard work will become easier and worth the effort. It will be less of a sacrifice and more of a joyous journey. It will not be as difficult to remain patient, to be persistent, and to not give up. When you're passionate about your book, your belief will convince others. It will make them into converts, supporters, and disciples who will deliver your message. Inspired by your passion and belief, they will help you build a groundswell for your book.

Don't give up. Innumerable books that were repeatedly rejected, shopped from publisher to publisher, have gone on to great success. All it takes is one publisher, one break, one "yes" to launch a book. Keep at it until you get that yes. We could provide story after story of books that were declined by numerous publishing houses before getting their chance to become International best-sellers. They are around every corner and hide in every nook and cranny. And to think if the authors took "no" for an answer the first time they heard it.

Publishing is a copycat industry; houses identify the types of books that are successful and try to determine how to capitalize on that success. They're always on the lookout for new interests and trends, and then they try to jump on the bandwagon. Why try to reinvent the wheel when they can just copy it?

As a result, many strong, inventive book ideas are rejected because the publishing industry is simply not ready for them; these books and ideas are before their time; they don't fit neatly into the required mold. Be patient and don't get discouraged. In time, the industry will catch up to you. A well-executed idea will always shine through.

Hang in there until the powers that be in the publishing industry see the light. Don't let the fact that they say no stop you. With each rejection, offer them more.

"When they say 'no,' I say, 'Well, let me give you another thing to think about before you hang up,'" Diane Shader Smith, author of *Undressing Infidelity* (Adams Media, 2005), reports. Be forceful, assertive. Take the attitude that nobody is going to stop you. Understand that you may get rejections, but see them as detours, not defeats. Find other routes, other targets, and keep moving forward. Be patient and understand that acceptance may take time.

Action Items

1. List your expectations for your writing and examine whether each is realistic.
2. Explain why it's important for writers to constantly read.
3. What is a brain dump and what are its pros and cons?
4. Explain why a book is always a work in progress.
5. Why must authors be passionate about their books?

·············· **REMEMBER** ··················

Writers have many options that they can take. Start writing. Set aside time each day to sit down and write, even if it's for only ten or fifteen minutes. Get into the habit of writing regularly, and don't worry about the quality of what you produce. Create a plan, but understand that writing is always subject to change. Like meetings and appointments, writing is something that should be, and can be, scheduled each and every day.

Dig deep to find the actual reasons why you want to write your book because they can influence the choices you make and the direction you chart.

Create a step-by-step plan. Think about the best way to get information and understand your topic, how you can find out what you should read and whom you should interview. Assess the competition, learn how you differ, and identify your niche.

Chapter 3

························

THE BIG IDEA

························

You can't wait for inspiration. You have to go after it with a club.
—Jack London

This chapter covers:
- Capturing ideas
- Substance and focus
- Write what you know
- Write what you want to learn
- Write what stirs your passion
- Write what interests others
- A new approach
- Test your idea

Ideas are the motors that drive nonfiction books. Often, it's the book idea, the promise of what will come, that most fascinates publishers and readers and gets them to buy books. Terrific ideas stimulate thought, excitement, and curiosity and make people want to read books. So before you try to write a single word, make sure that the concept for your book is not just good, but great.

Your book idea must be outstanding because it will help generate the energy that you will need to move forward and take all the steps necessary to actually write the book. Your idea can spur others to support your book, to talk it up, to promote it, and to help make it a big hit.

Ideas and inspirations for books are everywhere; they're triggered by an unlimited array of sources. Malcolm Gladwell, who wrote the best-selling *Blink: The Power of Thinking Without Thinking* (Little, Brown, 2005), gets his ideas from random places; he doesn't have a system. "I'm sort of a magpie. People tell me things or I read them and then follow up. I collect little bits, pieces and stories. Then, I go back and follow them up. I make it a point to try to talk to as many people from as many disparate places as possible and kind of try to pick their brains. I don't think that there is any formal way of doing it; it's a very social process," Gladwell discloses.

"When I come across a wonderful story, I try to marry that story to a broader theme or concept," Gladwell explains. "When I have a great idea or concept, I try to find a narrative to go along with it. A lot of what I do is matching stories and ideas. I've sat on wonderful stories for years before I found a way to use it or visa versa. I like to write things that have both of those features: have a kind of story and a kind of intellectual component. That means I have to be patient sometimes."

"Just open up your eyes, your ears and your heart and you'll see them," Dr. Dan Baker, coauthor of *What Happy People Know* (St. Martin's Griffin, 2004), advises. Much of what you see, if presented well, could make an interesting book. For example, you could write about your observations; a subject that has been your lifelong passion; people or events that intrigue you; what you do as a career, hobby, or quest; or a topic that you want to learn. Your book idea could be generated by your experiences; problems you've learned to solve; new methods you've perfected; a word, picture, or incident that trips the book-writing receptors in your brain.

"Keep your antennae up, keep watching for openings and opportunities, and things will happen," Louis Patler suggests. "Position yourself to see opportunities and take advantage of them when they arise."

Jay Conrad Levinson, creator of the best-selling Guerrilla Marketing series, gets his ideas from reading and constant research. "I see what other people are doing and how they're doing it and I research into marketing and entrepreneurs. I really don't consider it research because it's part of my natural curiosity," Levinson relates. "I look for new ideas and information that are not too technical and won't be too difficult for the average business operators to understand. I also look for established ideas and approaches that can be used in new ways."

Arthur H. Bell, author of forty-seven books, including *You Can't Talk to Me That Way: Stopping Toxic Language in the Workplace* (Career Press, 2005), finds inspiration from his dual careers as both a business professor and a consultant. In both capacities, he looks for problems he can solve and then writes about them.

Mary Roach's blockbuster *Stiff: The Curious Lives of Human Cadavers* (W. W. Norton & Company, 2004) grew out of a column she wrote for Salon.com. The idea for one of her other books, *Spook: Science Tackles the Afterlife* (W. W. Norton & Company, 2005), was triggered by a sentence she read in an article. Judi Culbertson's book *Scaling Down: Living Large in a Smaller Space* (Rodale, 2005) was suggested to her by her coauthor, Marj Decker, because "it could help lots of people."

After authoring *Outliers*, Malcolm Gladwell said, "I write books when I find myself returning again and again, in my mind, to the same themes. I wrote *The Tipping Point* because I was fascinated by the sudden drop in crime in New York City—and that fascination grew to an interest in the whole idea of epidemics and epidemic processes. I wrote *Blink* because I began to get obsessed, in the same way, with the way that all of us seem to make up our minds about other people in an instant—without really doing any real thinking. In the case of *Outliers*, the book grew out of a frustration I found myself having with the way we explain the careers of really successful people. You know how you hear someone say of Bill Gates or some rock star or some other outlier—'they're really smart' or 'they're really ambitious?' Well, I know lots of people who are really smart and really ambitious, and they aren't worth 60 billion dollars. It struck me that our understanding of success was really crude—and there was an opportunity to dig down and come up with a better set of explanations."

Some book ideas pop into your mind seemingly out of nowhere, and from that moment, all signs tell you that the idea is special and unique. You have no doubt about it and can't wait to dig in and start writing. Other ideas take ages to develop and form. Frequently, they're outgrowths of writers' interests, their focus and expertise in particular topics. Authors' inspirations may come from diverse sources for each of their books.

Author Jeff Greenwald traced the origin of the ideas for five of his books for us. They all grew from different seeds.

- His first book, *Mr. Raja's Neighborhood* (John Daniel & Company, 1986), came from a collection of letters he sent to friends when he was living in Nepal for a year. Greenwald didn't have a book in mind when he wrote the letters, but friends recognized that they would make a good book.
- The second book, *Shopping for Buddhas* (Harper & Row, 1990), began as a performance piece on stage. An editor from Harper and Row attended a performance and asked him to expand the piece into a book.
- Greenwald's third title, *The Size of the World* (Globe Pequot, 1995), came from his idea to write a book about traveling around the world without flying. So he wrote a proposal, sold the book, and spent nine months traveling around the world and another nine months writing the book.
- His fourth book, *Future Perfect* (Viking Penguin, 1998), came from an article he wrote for *Wired* magazine about the TV show *Star Trek*, which was the only TV show that allowed writers who were not professionals to pitch ideas and write screenplays.
- Greenwald's latest book, *Scratching the Surface: Impressions of Planet Earth from Hollywood to Shiraz* (Regent Press, 2002),

is a collection of stories he wrote as a travel writer over the course of twenty-five years.

- Now, he's working on a novel and, of course, toying with a number of other book ideas.

Seth Godin takes "cold showers until I come up with a neologism or two that describes something previously undescribed. Then I tell stories from real life that establish the truth of the issue in an emotional way. I almost never set out to write a book . . . it's forced upon me."

Romance writer Gregory Godek tells us, "I live in the context of the topic I write about. So when I read newspapers, magazines, see things on TV or make other observations, they're filtered through my interests. We all have a different focus. When an architect walks into a hotel, he probably focuses on how it looks, its color and design, not the quality of the service, how easy it is to check in or the nature of the other guests."

Godek, like many other writers we interviewed, always has three or four books in various stages in his mind. So he continually gathers information, and what usually happens is that one particular idea or phrase will jump out. "Phrases are everything; ideas and concepts become crystallized in phrases," Godek declares. "These phrases become book titles, which often are what agents, editors, publishers and readers buy."

When writers become intrigued by an idea, their curiosity usually takes over. A seed has been planted in their brain and they see everything in terms of their book idea. Suddenly, connections appear, all roads lead to their idea, and they consciously start looking for information on the topic.

Capturing Ideas

Ideas and inspiration can be fleeting; so many writers religiously carry pads or notebooks and stash them throughout their homes, offices, and vehicles so they can jot down any thoughts or information that may arise. Godek constantly carries a pad with him. He has one by his bedside and carries a two-inch pen in his wallet. "I've been known to interrupt almost anything to write down some idea because they're fleeting. It may not come back so you better capture it, write it down. Recently, I got a digital recorder as a public service to the other drivers of Southern California."

Leonard Koren, author of *The Flower Shop* (Stone Bridge Press, 2005) and over thirteen other books, always carries a pen and a few folded sheets of paper, on which he can jot down ideas and information. He walks frequently and finds it a particularly fruitful time for epiphanies. Although most of them turn out to be "of no use whatsoever," Koren tries to capture them when they occur because they can be useful. "It's a nice moment when you have a powerful insight or think that you have pinned something down," Koren states, "even though it turns out that you really didn't."

Writers often wake in the middle of the night with book ideas. So, many keep notepads and pens on their bedside table to capture them. Some report that their late-night insights tend to be very strong. Although they may be bleary-eyed when inspiration strikes, many have trained themselves to write nighttime notes clearly and in full, understandable sentences.

Robyn takes a notepad with her everywhere. When she has any downtime or is waiting, she makes notes on ideas for the books she is writing. She also stations a notepad on her nightstand for middle-of-the-night brainstorms. With the widespread use of smartphones, it is as easy as a push of a button to bring up a notepad and save your thoughts for later use. Today, you can even dictate and record reminders and messages that can be used to spark ideas at a later time.

When Laura Ries, coauthor of *The Origin of Brands* (Collins, 2004), is awakened by ideas, she will often get up and write. Frequently, she will write for hours, even to dawn, and produce high-quality work. In the quiet time between 3:00 A.M. and 9:00 A.M., she finds more clarity, less noise, and fewer interruptions.

When writers recognize that they have potentially good book ideas, they generally open files. Some keep a master computer file in which they list their book ideas along with comments and information about them. They may also open a hard file or folder for each book idea.

Some just let their ideas sit. They believe that if the idea stays with them, if they keep thinking about it for the next few weeks, it may have enough substance or power to develop into a book. However, other writers are less patient. They can't wait; when their good ideas strike, they feel compelled to immediately start developing them.

Substance and Focus

A book idea must be substantial enough to merit the writing of an entire book. If it's not, you'll end up padding and repeating, which will turn off readers. Thin book ideas also peter out quickly, as will your interest in writing about them. In no time, you will have written all that exists about the subject and have nothing to add. If your idea isn't substantial enough to hold your interest, your readers are bound to get bored. The flipside is that you should focus your concept and streamline it to ensure you are not writing a treatise or academic book on a specific subject. Non-fiction works should be long enough to take your reader on a journey and support personal growth, but not so long that it feels overwhelming and like a never-ending read.

"It's important to differentiate between an idea that is sufficient for a book and one that is only enough for an article," David Fryxell, author of *Write Faster, Write Better* (Writers Digest Books, 2004), explains. "Many ideas are not deep enough for a book-length work. When you develop them, there may not be that much to say. On the flip side, ideas must be focused. The whole point of writing nonfiction is focus. So figure out what part of an idea to focus upon. Some ideas are too big, they have to be cut down and controlled." It's like pruning the plants in your garden: you must cut out the weaker or dead growth so the stronger growth can thrive. If you don't cut out the excess and inessentials, you risk suffocating the plant.

Fryxell worked with a woman who was writing a memoir about the early days of rock and roll. However, she began her book with the story of her parents' courtship, which had nothing to do with the essence and most interesting part of the book. The focus of her book should have been her rock-and-roll experience, not her parents' romance, and when she realized it, she had to throw out about three hundred pages that she had already composed.

Super-agent John Willig shares the following thoughts on substance and focus: "All too often new authors are trying to appeal to a very broad range of potential readers vs. being focused on a specific theme and target audience that can be identified by their professional associations and groups. Key searchable words are important to include in titles and subtitles so editors will be able to quickly discern the category and potential buyers. The first 'sell' is to your potential editor who is overwhelmed with over-used and generic words and phrases, so in order to get his attention be specific. Don't try to be too 'cute' or 'sexy' as there will be enough time down the publishing road for all of that."

Author 101 Advice

Determine the focus of your book; isolate its core and single out your big idea and purpose. What is your book about? Identify the benefit your book will provide. How will your book help readers? Think about books that have impacted your life and how they made such a strong impression.

A nonfiction book must provide a benefit. Whether it gives information, provokes thought, or entertains by presenting a serious view or a hilarious spin on life, nonfiction must engage readers in your literary adventure. But also make sure you think of the bigger picture. A book can be so much more than a book. Mega-Agent and Story Merchant, Ken Atchity, has made his career by looking at the bigger picture. He has turned dozens of inspirational and motivational books into movies. He said, "Though I've observed the phenomena for several decades now, it still surprises me that even best-selling novelists, even the ones who complain that no one has made a film from their books yet, don't write novels dramatic enough to lend themselves easily to mainstream film. So time and again we read novels that start out well, roar along to the halfway point, and then peter off into the bogs of formless character development or action resolution. In today's world, a traditional publisher invests between $25,000 and $100,000 or more in publishing your novel. A low-budget feature film from a major Hollywood studio today costs at least $60 million; even in the independent world decent films can cost $2 to $5 million. There is, from a business point of view, *no* comparison between the book business and the film business in that regard. Risking $60 million means the critical factor is raised as high as can be imagined when your book hits the "story department"—much higher than the critical factor of even the finest publishers. Hollywood *studies* what audiences want by logging in box office dollars, cents, and surveys, what they respond best to. Whether your book is fiction or nonfiction, it needs to be shaped as a story if it's going to make it to the big or little screen. If you *structure your nonfiction book* dramatically even before you write the book, it'll no doubt be a better, reader-friendlier book and be destined for bigger opportunities."

Jeff Greenwald knows that an idea is substantial enough for a book (and even a movie) because it "rings a chord, it resonates, has a hook and enough layers of interest so that you know that you yourself won't get bored in the process of writing it." Greenwald states, "That's a key—if you get bored writing it, it's going to be very evident to anyone who tries to read it."

Essentially, you know from the sum of your experience, your reading, and your instincts when an idea is enough for a good book. This is another example of why reading is so important because by reading, you learn when ideas are sufficient to sustain an entire book and when they're insufficient.

Despite the success of some small books, most traditional publishers prefer to publish books that run more than two hundred pages or 40,000 words. They are concerned with perceived value and fear that most purchasers will see smaller books as having less value or potential impact on their lives. Whether or not this view is correct, it's what many publishers believe, and it influences their acquisition decisions. So, if you want your book to be published by a traditional publisher, understand that it may have to be of a sufficient size and depth.

Stedman Graham, author of *Diversity: Leaders Not Labels* (Simon & Schuster, June 2006), always has a number of book ideas in his mind. He is always thinking about the next project. He always asks how he can expand, about quality control and building a strong base or foundation. He is well organized and tries to take on projects with depth to maintain top quality. You also need a vision regarding where you want to go.

The ideas for Al and Laura Ries's books don't occur from a sudden flash of inspiration. They generally build over a long period of time. For example, Al analogized marketing to warfare in 1977, but *Marketing Warfare* (McGraw Hill, 1986), which he wrote with Jack Trout, didn't come out until 1986. So it took nine years for the idea to germinate. In those eight years, "You keep your eyes open for information on that idea," Ries declares. "For example, you also may write articles, make notes and start files on your idea—so by the time you start writing the book, you've collected a lot of material on the subject."

Dr. Brene Brown, Author of *Daring Greatly: How the Courage to Be Vulnerable Transforms the Way We Live, Love, Parent, and Lead* (Gotham, 2012) discussed with Oprah Winfrey how she came up with the idea for her best seller. "So one day I sent my husband, Steve, to work, I sent my kids to school, and I sat on the couch in my pajamas and watched ten hours of *Downton Abbey*. I ate some peanut butter. I didn't want to go back to my world, where all that hurt was. So instead I started googling to find out what was happening in the United States during the *Downton Abbey* period. That's when I found the Theodore Roosevelt quote. He said, 'It is not the critic who counts; not the man who points out how the strong man stumbles, or where the doer of deeds could have done them better. The credit belongs to the man who is actually in the arena, whose face is marred by dust and sweat and blood; who strives valiantly; who errs.... [And] if he fails, at least fails while *Daring Greatly*.' In that moment, my life changed. You know when you hear something and you're just ready?"

My Favorite Part

Stedman Graham loves coming up with concepts that can make great books; it's his favorite part of the book-writing process. Graham is a conceptual person. His strengths are innovation and creativity. He loves to put the pieces together and make sure that they flow the right way. In his book projects, he is the creator and the manager, "a multitasker who brings a lot of pieces to the table."

Write What You Know

The standard advice to aspiring writers is "write what you know," and it certainly makes sense. Unless you're a truly extraordinary mind, a poet, a philosopher, or a brilliant humorist, few people will want to read what you think. Many, however, may be eager to learn what you know.

If you've spent the bulk of your career in a particular field, you probably are an expert in that field or some sub-segment of it. Your expertise is valuable not only to your clients or customers, but also to the readers you can reach through books. Writing about your expertise can establish you as an authority in your field and boost your career because people love to do business and spend time with the person "who wrote the book." It infers that they are affiliated with the best.

When most nonfiction readers buy your books, they want your knowledge; they want solid information and clear guidance that they can use to solve their problems. Unlike turning on the radio or television, reading a book takes effort and commitment. So, when readers invest time and money in reading most nonfiction, they want practical information that will tell them, step-by-step, how to get concrete results; they want methods that work.

Find viable book ideas by:

- Making a list of problems in your field that you have repeatedly fixed and can clearly explain how you did so to readers
- Choosing issues that you know inside out
- Considering your daily activities and the topics you cover with your colleagues
- Selecting problems that affect many people or, alternatively, that address a smaller audience that will pay a premium to solve their particular problems
- Providing solutions that readers can implement themselves

Deliver what you promise and nothing less. If a book so much as hints that it will provide an answer, that is what it must do or readers will feel deceived, shortchanged, or ripped off. Remember, when you write a book, you are entering into a contract with your prospective audience. They purchase your book and you make them a promise to deliver a result. That result may be self-improvement, education, or an inspirational message. If you view your relationship with your readers as a contract, it will help you to take this relationship seriously and ensure you make good on that agreement. When authors don't deliver, the word spreads, and readers who feel that they have been burned won't buy your books. In fact, they might even complain about them.

Rick Says

Publishing a book on what you know can increase your visibility as an authority in your field. It can give you credibility with your colleagues and potential customers or clients. You will get invitations to speak at workshops and industry events where you can hobnob and do business with the movers and shakers in your field. At these events, you will get information from other authorities and from the questions and comments of event attendees that will also increase your expertise.

"When you have theories or ideas, give practical examples so readers can understand and identify with them," Collins Hemingway, coauthor of *Business @ the Speed of Thought* (Diane Publishing Company, 1999), notes. "For example, if you're writing a business book, give examples of your ideas in a real business context or people are likely to miss the point."

Write What You Want to Learn

Charles Cerami's approach to book ideas is to seize upon subjects that interest him and about which he wants to learn more. His acclaimed book on the Louisiana Purchase, *Jefferson's Great Gamble* (Sourcebooks, 2003), came from his reading. He found that books he read on the subject didn't cover the actual negotiations of the Louisiana Purchase and the men who conducted them. He was fascinated by what those books omitted, so he conducted research and decided that his findings would make an interesting book.

"When I am trying to get an idea for a book," Cerami explains, "I just walk up and down the aisles of my favorite libraries and pick up books that interest me. I see if they appear to be well done and exciting or if they are just full of facts and not otherwise very interesting. Then I ask if something interesting could be made of it. You must be fascinated by the subject you write about. If you find it dull, forget about it."

Writing isn't just about informing and explaining, it's also about discovering, exploring, and finding out. Many people choose writing as a career because they love to learn. Although learning is usually involved in all writing projects, some writers are drawn to projects that involve subjects they know little about because it requires them to study and learn. Collaborator and Book Architect Justin Spizman (www.justinspizman.com) told us, "Because I only take a limited number of projects at one time, I always ensure there is some wonder surrounding a book before I accept it. It is important that I am passionate about the subject, connect with the author, and am curious to learn more. Generally if I feel that way, so will the general audience. One of the most rewarding parts of my job is that I have the unique and distinct opportunity to learn directly from an expert about a topic I may not already know much about."

For these individuals, writing is the proof that they have successfully learned because it's impossible to write books on subjects that you don't really know. You may be able to bluff your way through an article or a short essay, but not through an entire book. Readers, editors, and publishers can spot a lack of knowledge in nothing flat.

Many writers like to lose themselves in their subjects and master them. Their need to understand their topic motivates them not only to educate themselves, but also to write books. Frequently, they write their books in the sequence in which they learned. So, in many ways, they're telling the story of how they learned. However, they usually emphasize the information rather than themselves or their experience.

Leonard Koren tries to understand the subjects of his books in new and different ways. He considers those subjects to be "very minor and almost could be considered trite," but he tries to get a different handle on the ordinary. If a book project takes two years, he may struggle during the first year and a half to get a handle on the subject matter, but then it clarifies itself.

When Koren begins working on a book, he doesn't know what his destination will be. He knows only that he wants to explore a certain terrain. His most notable success, *Wabi-Sabi: For Artists, Designers, Poets & Philosophers* (Stone Bridge Press, 1994), started when he was bored and began taking photographs. "Instead of thinking, I let my intuitive visual sense take over and direct me to what I found interesting to look at," Koren relates. For *Gardens of Gravel and Sand* (Stone Bridge Press, 1994), Koren photographed the gravel and sand in Kyoto's temples. He says of when he took those photographs, "I still didn't know what it meant. It took me a long time to realize that I was going to do a book on that particular subject."

He calls his process a kind of self-discovery. One of his earlier books, *The Flower Shop*, was inspired when he entered a flower shop as a tourist in Vienna and was attracted to it. When he first saw it, it was closed, so he went back another day and had an interesting conversation with the staff. Something about it intrigued him, but he didn't know what. It wasn't until months later, after he asked the owner if he could sit in the shop and observe, that he understood that there was "something here to make a book, but I didn't know exactly what. I knew that if I sat there and observed, I could probably make a book out of it— whatever it was that emerged."

Unquestionably, the hardest part for Koren is finding his way toward knowing what he's working on. It's a self-journey because he wants to make a book on the subject that no one else could. "If anyone else could do this book, I have this profound feeling that it would be a waste of my time. So it has to be something that only I could do because of my experience, the way my brain works, my intelligence, my aesthetic sensibility," Koren explains.

Writing what you want to learn is also a part of writing what you know because as you're providing information, you're also learning what you don't know. So, to make your writing complete, you must investigate what you don't know in order to present the full story.

A drawback of Koren's approach is that it's difficult for him to write book proposals. "In book proposals, I have to pretend that I know what my books will be at the end. I've always envied people who seem to have a firm idea of what they're going to do in the beginning and who structure it and zip, write a book."

Katherine Ramsland thinks that she conveys a sense of discovery when she's writing about information she just learned. At this point, she can play with language and find the right words to capture information and feelings, which she thinks is the "fun and the craft of writing. This is when writers can see how closely they can describe the totality of their feelings for the experience."

Write What Stirs Your Passion

"You must be very passionate about your book ideas," David Fryxell, author of *Write Faster, Write Better* (Writers Digest Books, 2004), explains. "Writing a book is a lot of work, it takes a lot of time and commitment, so you have to really care deeply about your core idea. People often get excited about book ideas, but when they try to write the books, they don't follow through."

When we interviewed authors for this book, they stressed the importance of passion. "If you're focused on what your passion is," Stedman Graham points out, "you're really aware of what you should be doing in your life and you understand your purpose; you're always looking for opportunities to build that passion."

Since it takes lots of work and information to complete even the smallest, most basic book, it's essential for writers to find ways to motivate themselves. This is where passion plays a leading role. Passion is an unparalleled motivator; it's a fire that drives you to succeed. Passion is more than interest, enthusiasm, or excitement; it's an intense, burning desire that borders on compulsion and challenges the limits of your self-control.

Robyn has always been passionate about writing thank-you notes and wrote a book about them, *The Thank You Book* (Active Parenting Publishers, Second Edition, 2004). Since Robyn's book addressed only adults, her daughter Ali, who is now in her late twenties, wrote *The Thank You Book for Kids* (Active Parenting Publishers, 2002) when she was twelve. For inspiration, Ali wrote famous people like Michael Eisner and asked him who taught him to say thank you, and she wrote the president of Harvard and asked if Harvard teaches students to say thank you. When you're passionate about a topic, it's a joy to write about it, and readers appreciate and support it.

Writing a book isn't easy. It is a journey that takes dedication and determination. The graveyard of unfinished books is growing by the second. The undertaking of authoring a book is not a simple and time savvy endeavor. It can literally take a village. Having wonderful ideas and wanting to share or display your knowledge may simply not be enough to get you past the hurdles you will face. And the process can be demoralizing because at every juncture people may criticize or diminish what you've written or plan to write.

Agents and editors will critically question your content and every word you write. Your friends, family, and associates, in the guise of being constructive, will have no compunction about telling you what you should write and how it should be written. People who never read books, and write even less, will tell you what you should write. And in doing so, they all may try to strengthen their arguments by belittling your ideas or your writing.

In addition, self-editing, which is an inherent part of writing, can wear down even the most accomplished authors. Occasions will arise when what you've written doesn't work, isn't clear, is out of order, or makes no sense. Vital information that you've built several chapters around may be missing or incorrect, and spotting the problem and finding a cure can be elusive. When you realize the amount of work fixing it will take, it may make you feel like quitting.

To stay with it, to persevere, to avoid the land mines and complete your book, you need passion. You must believe in your work and feel so strongly about the value of your book that nothing presents a problem that you can't overcome.

Write What Interests Others

The purpose of books is to communicate, and the purpose of nonfiction books is to convey knowledge, insights, and understanding to others. It's an exchange that involves two parties: writers and readers. Without interested readers, writing a book can be less satisfying and may even be an empty exercise with few rewards.

Passion, as we just discussed, can be a dynamic motivator, but it can also be blinding. In our passion about our subjects and books, we can be so convinced of the value of our writing that we don't see the other side. Our passion can be completely misplaced, and in truth, few readers may be interested in our book.

When you begin to write a book, it's always desirable to start with exciting ideas because they hold your interest and motivate you. But you must also determine if others will be interested in what you want to write. Try to identify, as precisely as possible, who your audience will be and its size. Don't delude yourself into thinking, as many writers do, that your book will have universal appeal.

A very easy way to do some quick market research is to spend some time on Amazon.com. Amazon has graciously categorized all the books they sell, along with the number of books in each specific category and their overall rankings, based on the number of books sold. Thus, it only takes a few clicks of your mouse to obtain a general view of the types of books that are being published and more importantly, being purchased.

When you write what interests others, you get two major advantages:

- It identifies the market for your book, which agents and publishers want to know, and if that group or groups is large, it can influence the advance that you may receive.

- It will improve your writing and the focus of your book. When you know who your readers will be, what they have in common, what they do, what they buy, what they need, and what they like and dislike, it will help you direct your efforts toward that precise audience.

If you find that the book you want to write does not interest others, it's often easy to make small adjustments that will widen its appeal. Regardless, before you start writing, take the time to gain a clear understanding as to the size of your market; the bigger the market, the larger the opportunity for sales. That doesn't mean you should write your book solely for a large market. But it does mean you should consider your potential market as part of your research before you put pen to paper or fingers to keyboard. Agents and editors are sharply attuned to the audiences for books, so solicit their advice and seriously consider making the changes they suggest.

My Least Favorite Part

For Collins Hemingway, the least favorite part of the book-writing process is the writing. Hemingway finds research fun; he loves studying and learning. When you write a book, "It isn't sufficient to just find two or three seminal articles or books on a topic and then simply recapitulate them," Hemingway notes. "For a book, you must also summarize what you read and add something new on top of it. It requires deep thinking because after you've done your reading and research, you always have to think about what you have and ask what's new about it."

A New Approach

"An idea itself doesn't make a book. What you really need is an angle and a focus," David Fryxell states. "Figure out what part of the story you're going to tell, where you should start and how far you should go. Then what angle or approach you're going to take."

Since most book ideas are not new, their presentation must be unique. It isn't about the gift, but rather, it is about the gift-wrapping. Acknowledging that you are not reinventing the wheel is important. But you do have to take the time and put forth the energy to separate your book from others on the market. That can be done through presenting a common idea in an uncommon package. Neither publishers nor readers want books on subjects that say the same old thing in the same old way. However, they may be interested in books that state old ideas differently and with new, improved, or fresh angles, perspectives, or slants. So think about presenting your idea in a new format, or in light of or in comparison with new or different information. Or you could write about an old idea for a new audience.

When Diane Shader Smith, author of *Undressing Infidelity* (Adams Media, 2005), was tempted to have an affair, she decided to first investigate infidelity before she got irrevocably involved. Smith talked with other women, checked out bookstores, and read girlfriends' guides. She found loads of books about infidelity, but none written in the first person or in an uncensored, nonjudgmental style, which became the approach for her book. Smith was able to get her book published because she could differentiate it from those that had already been published in a successful market.

Robyn Says

Ideas come from many places, so you have to be open and aware of topics that just might create a fabulous book. When you become a writer, you begin to see the world through new eyes. You sense what would make a great book, and it propels you to write it. Ask yourself, "Does the world need one more book on this subject? If the answer is no, then head in a different direction."

When you do your homework, it is usually obvious if the Internet and bookstores are already flooded with books on your topic. If you see the need for a book, however, you can build a better case for writing it. When I think of a book idea that is fresh and hasn't been overdone, I feel captivated by the essence of that book, and I have to write it and bring it to life.

"Be careful not to differentiate merely for the sake of differentiating in order to justify writing the book," Florence M. Stone, author of over fifteen books, including *The Essential New Manager's Kit* (Kaplan Education, 2003), warns. "If this occurs, you may not have a good book idea. Publishers check Amazon."

Test Your Idea

Ideas can be magical; they can be brilliant, revolutionary, and hysterical. They can change the world. However, they can also be impractical, unrealistic, or just plain dumb, especially with the intervention of time. It's hard to be objective about your own ideas, especially those that you feel passionate about. And determining whether your idea is good enough for a book that a publisher and readers will buy can be especially difficult. So test your book ideas.

David Shenk, author of *The Genius in All of Us: New Insights into Genetics, Talent, and IQ* (Anchor, 2011) recommends to: "Get feedback—oodles of it. Along the way, show pieces of your book to lots of people—different types of people. Ply them with wine and beg them for candor. Find out what's missing, what's being misinterpreted, what isn't convincing, what's falling flat. This doesn't mean you take every suggestion or write the book by committee. But this process will allow you to marry your necessarily precious vision with how people will actually react. I find that invaluable."

"When picking a subject, wait until you're completely fascinated with it," Charles Cerami suggests. "Don't be too worried that other books have been written on the subject, especially if you can find a unique or different angle or approach, because the existence of those books shows that there's interest in the subject."

Test your book ideas to determine if they're sufficient for an entire book. Many great ideas are simply not meaty enough for a book, even a short book. They may make gripping articles, but involve only one or two interesting points that can be covered without going into great depth. Create a one to two page summary of your book and send it to some of your respected friends or colleagues. Listen to their feedback and adjust accordingly. We all have strong critics in our lives, so take the strategic steps to use them. A book needs legs; it has to hold readers from beginning to end, not just engross them for a few early chapters and then put them to sleep.

Look for ideas that have depth, several layers, and can't be fully covered in a few pages. Ask whether your book idea involves questions and information that will hold both your and your readers' interest. Although ideas for books don't have to be overly complex, they must involve different facets that give the book substance and weight.

Personal Experiences

The idea for Alison James's *Better Off Wed?* (Polka Dot Press, 2006) originally came from her own experience. Then she checked with other women to see if she was the only one going through this experience. "You have to have a personal interest or reason for doing what you're doing. But at the same time, it has to appeal to a lot of other people," James points out. "Women want to know that what they're going through is normal, that other women are going through it also and you're not going to be locked away in an asylum." When James writes about women's common problems, their connections and shared curiosity, it comes through in her writing.

Knowing that an idea could become a book "is partially a science and partially an instinctive process," James observes. "And it's hard. It has to 'set right' with me; it has to feel right in my gut. I can't always figure out why some things set right and others don't. I read what's out there, what's on the Amazon bestseller list. I look at books that have done really well in other genres and figure out if there's a way to spin that same idea into my genre." James got the idea for her book *The 10 Women You'll Be Before You're 35* from Mitch Albom's *The Five People You Meet in Heaven*.

Eben Alexander, author of *Proof of Heaven: A Neurosurgeon's Journey into the Afterlife* (Simon & Schuster, 2012) writes from personal experience. "Before my 'near death experience' (NDE) I did not read any 'near death' literature because I didn't think that sort of thing could be real. I was very much a scientist who believed physics, chemistry, and biology explained everything in the world. I thought NDEs resulted from the chaotic ramblings of the dying brain…those ideas were crushed. So this is obviously is a *very deeply personal story*. Once I realized the power of my NDE in 2008, and what it was telling me—I knew I had to get it out there."

Pick What Already Works

Examine what has worked well in other places. In business, companies always look at what other businesses have done successfully and then they try to implement those methods that could work for them. Authors should do the same. So look for:

1. What has sold and what is selling
2. Why it sold
3. How you can make the success of others work for you

In testing your book ideas, also consider whether they (1) will be distinctive, (2) address an identifiable audience, and (3) have commercial potential. We will discuss these factors in the following chapter, Chapter 4, "Does a Market Exist?"

Stedman Graham's inspiration for his books has come from looking at the marketplace. He tries to identify the missing pieces in the consumer book market based on where the marketplace is going, and he writes books that are three to five years ahead of current trends in order to stay on the cutting edge.

Show the Idea Around

When Graham gets book ideas, he bounces them off all kinds of folks: people he is in contact with, his staff, friends, and business associates. He will call a contact and ask, "I have this idea, what do you think of it?" He got the idea for his latest book while he was doing business with an associate, so he ran the idea by his colleague to get his input. During conversations or business dealings, something might come up and Graham will say, "Wow, that could make an interesting book. I'd like to do something on that."

Graham tests his book in the marketplace. He runs it by groups at meetings, workshops, and personal appearances. If an audience likes an idea and provides feedback confirming that it's viable, Graham will take it to additional audiences. He will also tweak the idea according to the audiences' responses, to further refine the idea.

Author 101 Advice

Although you may not have access to groups as Graham does, you can imitate his approach. Assemble groups of your friends and associates; take them for breakfast or coffee and solicit their opinions about your ideas. Record the session or take detailed notes on the feedback you receive.

Test your book ideas on selected individuals, people whose judgment you respect. Speak with agents, editors, other writers, librarians, and people who work in bookstores. Literary agents are experts at evaluating book ideas, and they excel at offering suggestions that can strengthen your books. Don't be overly sensitive and recognize that this simple yet effective experiment can be the difference in creating a truly marketable and successful book or one that is simply falling flat.

"I bounce my ideas off my agent to get his opinion," Florence M. Stone states. "Then the most important part is to write the proposal and to compare what you propose to write with the books that are out there already. If you can't differentiate what you have in mind with what is already out there, it makes it even more difficult to write a book. So, when I'm developing a book, I'm looking for the ability to say that my book does this while all the other books that have been published only go in this direction."

Also run your book ideas past friends and associates who read frequently and who are involved in book clubs or publishing. Find a group of advisors, people with different interests and backgrounds, who will honestly tell you what they think of your ideas. Then carefully weigh their suggestions and advice.

Be wary about seeking advice from your close family and friends. In most cases, they won't be totally honest with you because of the closeness of your relationship. In addition, they may not have the type of knowledge you want about publishing and books.

Katherine Ramsland gets lots of ideas but has to make sure that they are "book worthy." She asks, "Is there enough here to write an entire book that would be full of useful information and provide an opportunity for me to learn? When I write a book, I want the stimulation and the momentum of finding out things as I'm going." Ramsland looks for projects that open her up and make her feel like she is getting a lot out of them.

Energy Leaks

Ramsland fears that prematurely revealing an idea can create what she calls an "energy leak." The mere fact that Ramsland has put energy into telling others about her idea, rather than writing about it, can, she believes, zap its power. So she has become protective of the potency of her ideas and will talk about them only after she has written and worked on them. Only then will Ramsland mention her ideas to others to see if they have particular thoughts on how she could direct, focus, or add to them.

Action Items

1. Explain why the idea for your book must be great.
2. List three reasons why you should write a book.
3. Why is it important for books to take new approaches?
4. How can writers test their book ideas?
5. What is meant by the term *energy leak*?

REMEMBER

Great book ideas are everywhere. They stimulate thought, excitement, and curiosity and make people want to read books. Authors get their ideas from what they know, what they want to know, what stirs their passions, and what interests others. Since most book ideas have been written about, they must be presented in a new and different way. But even then, the market can be unpredictable.

Malcolm Gladwell says he never knows what people will take from his books.

"It's never what I think it's going to be. Parts that you think are going to make this big impact are ignored, and parts that you wrote in a day are like the 10,000 hours stuff—I thought no one would ever mention that again. And it is, in fact, all people talk about. Who knew?"

When you come up with book ideas, they must be sufficient in scope to warrant the writing of an entire book. Since authors can be blind with regard to their own book ideas, they should test them by checking with agents, editors, other writers, and readers they respect. Find ways to test your book ideas. Draw up a list of friends and associates with whom you could discuss your book ideas.

Chapter 4

DOES A MARKET EXIST?

I have learned that success is to be measured not so much by the position that one has reached in life as by the obstacles which he has overcome while trying to succeed.
—Booker T. Washington

This chapter covers:
- Preliminary research
- Comparable works
- How is your book distinctive?
- Consult your agent
- Credentials

Publishing is a business; most publishers must earn money from their book sales to stay in business. So before they acquire books, publishers usually must believe that the books will sell, that they have identifiable markets. When authors pitch publishing houses to buy their books, the publishers expect the authors to submit book proposals that justify the potential markets for those books.

In order for writers to realistically assess how well their books will sell, they must understand how their books are unique and how they compare to books they will be competing with in the marketplace. Lena Dunham, creator of the popular show "Girls" on HBO, sold her book proposal to Random House for a reported $3.6 million dollars. She created a 66-page illustrated proposal that netted her approximately $56,000 per page. Her quirky and unique style was different than the style of most other writers out there, but she was confident that her ideas would be welcomed as exciting and novel. Susan Kamil, the editor-in-chief and publisher of Random House, said, "We're thrilled to welcome Lena to Random House. Her skill on the page as a writer is remarkable—fresh, wise, so assured. She is that rare literary talent that will only grow from strength to strength and we look forward to helping her build a long career as an author."

In other words, each author must understand his or her book's special niche and who will probably buy it. In addition to helping them to establish the market for their books, knowing their niche enables authors to focus their writing more directly. It helps them identify and emphasize their main points and distinguish them from the positions held by others. When authors identify their audience and what makes them unique, they can address them more precisely and more personally and keep their interest. "Writers are often confused about both who they are and who their market is," Arthur H. Bell reveals. "You need to have a clear picture about the kind of people who will read your book, their backgrounds, smarts and work experience. This impacts how you market to them, your choices of anecdotes, vocabulary and tone of voice because you have no firm basis upon which to make those decisions. Do you say 'mitigate' or do you say 'change'? You have to know that going in."

"One of the main problems is that many writers are introverted people who listen to inner voices," Bell believes. "They haven't been out there with big ears listening to others as extroverts do. While their inner voice is the writing voice, they can be writing for themselves. Extroverts, on the other hand, conduct conversations with others, not just with themselves. God gave us two ears and one mouth and they should be used in that proportion. So introverts have to be aware that they must turn on some sensing devices to the outside world. If they don't, they may write their one great work, but that will be it because they may not understand the world outside. Too many writers write for themselves, not for their readers. Unfortunately, the self is of limited interest and once you get a book or two written about yourself, it's pretty much the story." After Lois P. Frankel wrote *Nice Girls Don't Get the Corner Office* (Warner Business Books, 2004), her editor wanted her to write a follow-up on how women should handle their finances, which eventually became *Nice Girls Don't Get Rich* (Warner Business Books, 2005). Initially, Frankel questioned whether she wanted to, or was qualified to, write such a book, but she soon realized that many of the principles she believed also applied to women's finance issues. Dr. Frankel began checking similar books that had been published and found that a great deal had been written on financial planning for women, but none of it was on financial thinking and the psychology of women and money. So that became her niche. Authors must know their niche and how their books differ from others in the market in order to know whether their books will be commercially viable. If they hold themselves out as experts, they must also know their own area of expertise and everything else in the field, including the information in, and how their book will compare to, competitive books.

Preliminary Research

When your book idea is in its embryonic stages, before it's even taken full form, conduct preliminary research. First, search the Internet to get a sense of how much information on the subject is online, which usually indicates the level of interest in it.

Use your initial inquiry for two purposes:

1. To note the perspectives of the coverage
2. To gather additional knowledge on the subject

Research to find out:

- What materials exist or don't exist
- How others have approached the subject

- What others have stressed
- What others have omitted
- How thoroughly the subject has been covered

Make printouts or detailed notes of the information you find that you can keep in your files and use for later reference.

Read all items that could be directly on point and informative. Frequently, the content for entries that come up during Internet searches will not be as advertised. For instance, many that seem to be exactly on point may, upon closer reading, be far afield. However, entries that appear questionable or even irrelevant could contain valuable gems. As you explore, look to see if any items cover information or insights that you planned to cover. Also see what other leads these entries provide and follow them.

Check online booksellers' sites for information about books on the subject. These sites usually describe and review books—but don't put too much stock in the reviews they post. People may have written them to make the authors' books look good, or they may just have different perspectives and objectives from yours.

Instead, use the online bookseller sites as secondary sources. Then go to bookstores or libraries to examine the books firsthand. Check the publication dates of all books of interest and see if you can sense any trends or directions in which the subject is heading. Frequently, progressions from book to book will help you identify what should be included in the next volume on the subject.

During your preliminary research, keep your options open and don't make any firm decisions. Consider your search to be an information-finding exploration. Print out material that could be useful to you, and organize it in folders or files. Then review everything that you collected to find the directions or slants that emerge.

When Jay Conrad Levinson has an idea for a book, he reads everything he can find about it. This phase can take Levinson several months. Mainly, he's looking for ideas and information that will help him develop a complete understanding of what is involved and how he can convey it clearly. He reads books, articles, and items on the Internet. "When I need information, I don't care where it comes from as long as it's reliable information," Levinson reports.

"I bring to my books, more than the research I've done, but also the life I've lived because I've spent so many years doing what I write about," Levinson explains. "As I write, I'm able to take the ideas I've identified for inclusion in the book and embellish them from my memory. I get into a flow, where I do nothing but write."

Rick Says

While you're online, search the proposed title of your book. If it's taken or if you find anything close, see how old those titles are. Since titles can't be copyrighted, books having identical titles are often published. If enough time has passed or an earlier book had small sales, you may still want to use your proposed title or make a minor change. If you use the same title, consider adding a subtitle that expresses the uniqueness of your book.

Also check if your proposed title has been used in a website address. Check it and similar URLs. If your title is available, reserve the address at *www.rickscheapdomains.com.*

Speaking of titles, looking at a number of book titles can help your writing and your book. It can sharpen your "headline sense" because titles and headlines are really one in the same. Plus, writing for today's readers should contain frequent headlines, subheads, and bulleted items, which are also a form of headlines, because they direct readers' attention to key material and make it easy for them to notice and retain major points.

When some writers conduct their preliminary research, they go through a more internal and personal process. Writers such as Joseph Cardillo, the author of *Bow to Life* (Avalon, 2006), look more into themselves, their experiences and feelings, than they do to outside sources. Cardillo writes about the Eastern martial arts from a personal perspective and most of his research is on himself. "I try to scoop out the experiences I've had, think about them, understand them and then see how they can be presented so that others can relate to and benefit from them," Cardillo explains.

My Favorite Part

Gregory Godek's favorite part of the writing process is writing a brilliant sentence or paragraph. "When you just sit there and say, 'Son of a bitch, I got it.' It's great; it's really accomplishing something. It's even better than finishing a book, because finishing a book includes both joy and sorrow," Godek states.

Comparable Works

Go to bookstores and libraries and browse through the stacks. Find and examine comparable or competitive books. Take them off the shelves and leaf through them and read selected portions. Get an understanding of the books' perspectives, how they're organized, and the type of information they contain.

Make notes on each book you examine. List their strong points, weak points, what you like about them, and what you dislike. Determine how you think your book will differ and how it will be better. Try to be honest and objective.

While you're in the stacks, look a bit further. At the least, note the titles of all the books on the self and those above and below them. Although those titles may not be directly on your subject, they can help you understand how authors have approached the general and closely related topic.

"Look at all the books you can read in your area. Organize your industry, know what's there, what they say," Stedman Graham recommends. "Know the top books that state how the process works, how to improve your writing and how to make your book better, more relevant and better written. Don't be tied to one book; organize the information around what you do and need as much as possible."

When publishers receive book proposals, they pay close attention to the section that analyzes comparable books. In this section, proposal writers list the books that they consider most similar to theirs, briefly describe them, and state how their books will differ.

Publishers place great weight on how writers handle this section because they want assurances that the writers know about the books that have been written in their fields and that the writers understand their own particular niches. They also want an overview of the precise competition the proposed book would face.

For publishing houses, publishing is a business, so they want as much information as possible on which books they will be battling for shelf space. Although publishers can easily research this information and will usually verify it for themselves, they want to be certain that the proposal writers are aware of the commercial and competitive aspects involved in the publication of their books.

Visit bookstores and libraries to learn what is on the shelves where your book would sit. Meet your potential neighbors and get to know them. As an expert in your field, you probably have already read some of your competition; now read the rest.

- Take notes on each comparable book's content, format, size, age, and price.
- See what printing they're in and try to discover how many copies each sold.
- Examine how each has treated similar ideas.
- List what you like, dislike, and what you can improve.
- Specifically note how your book will differ, how it will be better, and what new material or information it will contain.
- Determine if your book addresses the same audience or whether it takes a different twist.
- Ask whether the style or format of your book will differ, and if so, if that will be enough to distinguish it from existing books.
- Specify precisely what your book will contain that readers cannot get from similar books.
- Speak with bookstore staff members or librarians to discover what feedback they have received on similar books.

How Is Your Book Distinctive?

When publishers receive interesting book proposals, they bring them before in-house committees and editorial boards. These groups are composed of individuals from various in-house departments, including sales and marketing people. Since everyone at these meetings is involved with books, they tend to think in terms of comparable books, especially those that are currently on the market.

They will say, "Oh, is it like _____?" Or "What makes it different from _____?"

Publishers also are trend oriented, so they look to publish books that will build upon or capitalize on themes of successful books. For example, publishers rushed to get on the chick-lit bandwagon, and after the success of *The Da Vinci Code*, they clamored for similar books.

Many writers mistakenly think that the existence of comparable books is a strike against them, but the opposite may be true. The fact that similar books have been published can be advantageous for aspiring authors because it shows that a demand exists for that genre of book if the authors can give their books new or different twists.

Before publishers commit to acquiring a property, they often take proposals to buyers for the big bookseller chains to ask their opinions on the book's sales potential. So it's incumbent on writers to state in their proposals how their books will appeal to all of the readers that bought prior best-sellers. Agent John Willig offers a caveat: "Editors have to be great at managing expectations. If all you include in your competition section are best-sellers vs. solid performers then you are going to just raise red flags with them. While it's wonderful to think of your proposed book as the next bestseller in the field, the majority of books sell modest amounts and make additional money for publishers through selling subsidiary rights like foreign translations, audio books, digital formats, etc...."

Many writers believe that their ideas are unique, and they are also prone to exaggeration, which can offend agents, editors, and publishers. For example, aspiring authors may claim, "Nothing like my book has ever been written" or "This is the only book that has ever been written about _____." They will also inflate the potential market for their books by claiming that they will be blockbusters, best-sellers, and timeless classics.

Unfortunately, all of the above is seldom true. Your book invariably shares similarities with other books in some aspect whether it's theme, content, style, or format. When writers allege that their books are one of a kind, totally unique and unlike any other books, industry professionals bristle and feel that the writers haven't done their homework. The professionals may infer from the omissions that the writers will also be lax in writing their books.

Grandiose claims about books' sales potential also make the professionals shudder because they know that they probably won't even come close. It tells them that the writers have unrealistic expectations and that even if they make an offer to acquire the book, the writers may be offended and difficult to work with if they agree to do the book.

So, be realistic about your audience, and even if you think that your book will have wide appeal, identify the specific group or groups that would be most likely to read it. After you've identified your core readers, ask yourself what additions, twists, or changes you could make that would give your book broader appeal without weakening it.

Robyn Says

When you visit bookstores and libraries, introduce yourself to the staff and tell them about your project. Ask their opinions about your book idea and if they can recommend books or articles for you to read. Also find out which books on your subject are popular with readers.

People who work in bookstores and libraries are usually devoted and informed readers who love writing and books. They often know writers or people involved in publishing with whom they can connect you.

Jay Conrad Levinson doesn't worry about reading competitive works. He looks at them before he starts writing his books, but not while he's writing them. He knows that he's going to learn from almost any book he reads, but if he lets any of it intimidate him, he might never write another book. "In order to write, you must have a massive ego while you're writing. I don't want that ego trampled by superior writers. You have to really believe that you have something important to say," Levinson acknowledges.

At the library, search the periodicals. Speak with the reference librarian and get a list of articles you can review.

Florence M. Stone tells aspiring writers to "check the titles that specific publishers have released to find those that could be good for your book. Also check to see how well the similar books that those publishers have released have sold, because if they didn't do well, they may not be interested in your book.

Amazon and B&N frequently give the numbers of sales or how they ranked it. Also ask at bookstores what is selling well in your area."

My Least Favorite Part

Judy Ford, like most writers, hates when her editor says, "What are you talking about? You need an example here, you sound as if you're exhausted and just want to get it done." Writers often mistakenly feel that they have made themselves clear when actually they did not. So when an editor calls it to their attention they appreciate it, but it can be a bitter pill to swallow.

Consult Your Agent

Literary agents know the book market. They know what types of books are selling and what types are not. They excel at knowing how to make books more salable. Many have spent years working in publishing and have been acquisition editors, so they understand what publishers want and how and when they want it. Agents tend to nurture close ties with editors, publicists, other agents, and other industry professionals. Selling books is their profession, and many do it extremely well.

Scott Hoffman is a Founding Partner of Folio Literary Management, LLC, a NYC-based literary agency that has represented dozens of NY Times best-sellers since its founding in 2006.

He said, "In the past, the road to publication was clear, if not easy. If you wanted your book to be widely available, you had one path: find a literary agent who would represent you and sell your book to a big New York publishing house, which would ensure that it got to the physical stores where the vast majority of consumers bought their books. Authors themselves weren't qualified to talk directly to the Deities of Publishing, gods with names like Knopf and Scribner. But for a price, an agent would speak on their behalf. For a small group of authors and agents, the process worked well. Books were published, and fortunes were made, but the system left most out in the cold."

Hoffman then proceeds to discuss how the industry has significantly changed. He stated, "Over the past decade, however, the landscape has changed dramatically. With the advent of eBooks, direct-to-consumer publishing, and the emergence of entrepreneurial publishers, authors are no longer beholden to publishing behemoths. For a small percentage of authors, the massive financial resources and teams of world-class experts at major publishing houses still add tremendous value. And the agents who act as their advocates play a critical role in getting their message out and allowing writers to monetize their ideas. But the role of agent as gatekeeper is fast disappearing. Traditional publishers are beginning to draw more and more authors from the ranks of successful self-publishing, a trend that is bound to continue. Those agents who made a living by hording wisdom and controlling access are quickly seeing their niche in the ecosystem become obsolete. The most successful agents of the future will be the ones who share what they've learned with as many people as possible, empowering writers to spread their ideas to people who need them, and connecting the world through the power of the written word. The best agents will stop saying 'no,' and will find a way to say 'yes.' There is no other option."

Good agents are more than manuscript peddlers; they are brand and career builders and managers. They don't just want to sell their clients' books; they want to develop and grow their careers. They're not in it for quick sales, but to help create long writing careers. So agents can be invaluable advisors to their clients on book ideas.

An example of how author-agent relationships often work is as follows: When Charles Cerami gets an idea for a book, he bounces it off his agent, Bob Silverstein. He sends Silverstein a long e-mail laying out his idea and how he plans to expand it into a book. His agent, like most agents, is sharply attuned to the market and has strong instincts on what will and won't sell. Frequently, Silverstein will reject Cerami's book ideas because he doesn't think they will sell.

If Silverstein thinks that a subject that Cerami likes has potential, Cerami will try to write a chapter list to show how he would organize the book. He tries to give the chapters exciting names, and when he has about twenty-five assembled, he starts writing a sample chapter.

"When you send your proposal to your agent, you have to trust him or her to send it to the right publishers, to have an understanding of the market," Florence M. Stone explains. "So you want someone who knows a particular market well—and you have to trust his or her advice."

If you don't have an agent, speak with the staff members at local bookstores and libraries. They usually know the market and the public's reading interests. Frequently, they're deeply involved in writing and books and can offer insightful advice about the market for your book or on how you could improve your approach.

Also enlist friends who are readers, as well as colleagues and associates who may be involved in the fields on which you want to write. Solicit their opinions and request their advice, which could be extremely helpful.

Robyn Says

I always consult first with my literary agent to see what she thinks. She gives me very valuable feedback that helps me improve a book idea or add a spin that makes it better. An agent should be someone you brainstorm with, who sees the bigger picture and is dedicated to helping you grow as an author. It's not just about the next sale; it's also about where you want to go with your career.

Credentials

An author's credentials strongly affect his or her ability to sell his or her book. Readers want nonfiction books written by authors who have outstanding credentials, and publishers insist on them. You may be the best investigative reporter, but a publisher won't buy your health-care book unless you've spent years on the health-care beat or you coauthored it with a physician.

Credentials give authors credibility; they indicate to readers that an author is worth reading because he or she has spent years specializing in selling software in Asia, helping small businesses retain their employees, or installing home security systems.

"You need expertise because it establishes trust," Arthur H. Bell explains. "Once your credibility is established, you don't need to have more footnotes on a page than you have text. People are willing to let you talk within a book and will listen to what you say. Your personal physician speaks out of expertise in the office without having to open the medical encyclopedia to show you the page it came from every two minutes."

Lois P. Frankel feels that she made the mistake of not cementing her expertise early enough in her earlier books. "Readers need to quickly learn why you're the expert on your subject, why you're credible, and why they should listen to you," Frankel observes. Many writers are reluctant to blow their own horn, but they have to establish reasons for readers to pay attention to them. They don't have to brag; they can do it softly because as Frankel suggests, "A little can go a long way."

Credentials don't necessarily mean having a page full of degrees, although that wouldn't hurt. It means that you know what you're doing. That you have practical, not just theoretical, experience and a full understanding of your area—the problems, latest developments, and innovations in your field. Most important, it means that you know how to solve real and troubling problems.

Action Items

1. Why is it important for aspiring authors to know their special niche?
2. What should writers look for when they conduct preliminary research for their books?
3. List five questions writers should ask when they examine comparable books.
4. If you don't have an agent, whom should you ask about the market for your book?
5. What is the most important requirement for an author's credentials?

··············· **REMEMBER** ···················

Authors must know their special niche in order to focus their writing more directly, to stress their main points and distinguish them from positions held by others. Conduct preliminary research to learn how the subject of your book has been covered in other books and to gather additional knowledge and information on the subject.

Visit bookstores and libraries to examine comparable books. Learn about them and how your book will be different and better. Run your book ideas by your agent, people who work in bookstores and libraries, and trusted associates and friends. Make sure that you are qualified and have the practical experience to write the book you propose.

Chapter 5

....

CREATING AN
AWARD WINNING PROPOSAL

....

*Take up one idea. Make that one idea your life—think of
it, dream of it, live on that idea. Let the brain, muscles,
nerves, and every part of your body be full of that idea, and
just leave every other idea alone. This is the way to success.*
—Swami Vivekananda

This chapter covers:
- The Importance of a Proposal
- Creating the Proposal
- Securing an Agent
- Understanding the Process

The Importance of a Proposal

Proposal writing is certainly an acquired skill. But it is also a necessary one. Publishers receive thousands of proposals each and every month. In fact, most large publishing houses receive tens of thousands of annual submissions. They skim through most, and select only a few to truly "dive" into. And even those can be quickly discarded if the publishers are not immediately captured and interested. Needless to say, it is a tough world out there. One small error or strategic mistake or misstep can be the difference between a book deal and your manuscript gathering dust in a pile on a publisher's desk. Proposals are a learned trade and one you should work to perfect before blasting your book to potential publishers. The truth is that you may only get one shot or opportunity to make an impression and draw in potential publishers and editors for further review.

John Willig, successful agent and founder of Literary Services, Inc. says, "It's important for authors to understand that the proposal is an investment document and plan for publishers. Every day editors are presented many opportunities on how they are going to commit their company's resources and whom they are going to publish based on the appeal and clarity of the proposal presentation. Besides being expert wordsmiths and creative crafters of books, editors are also venture capitalists that have to sell your work internally to their group of decision-makers in publicity and marketing. So highlighting in your proposal how you are going to be great partner for them and produce profit is essential."

So with that in mind, our goal in this chapter is to discuss not only how to create an award winning book proposal, but also offer insight into publisher's expectations and how they make their buying decisions. It is rare for an author, new or old, to receive an offer without a publisher first reviewing the blueprint for his manuscript. Even a seasoned vet is required to submit at least a micro-proposal outlining the book's concept, the opportunity, and the marketing and advertising platform. No one gets a pass.

Terry Whalin, acquisitions Editor for Morgan James and author of over 60 books, shared with us that, "At any given time according to publishing experts, there are more than a million proposals and manuscripts which are in circulation. A well-crafted proposal has critical publishing decision-making information that never appears in a manuscript. Editors and agents are busy people and receive thousands of submissions. You only get one chance to make a good first impression. An editor is going to make a decision about your proposal in seconds. If you want to find your champion to promote your project inside the publishing company then you need to have a complete well-crafted proposal targeted for a particular group of readers that contains some fresh insights and information. I've written many proposals—two of which garnered a six-figure advance from publishers. Yet I understand they are hard work and can be as time consuming as writing the full manuscript."

Publishing houses look at books as investment opportunities. They have limited funds and even more limited resources to invest in projects. Thus, they need to make their purchases count. So, you will find publishers are stingy with offers and truly want to understand and scrutinize every last angle before they are willing to make an offer. Viewing the process through that lens will only help you to evaluate and understand the importance of an interesting, engaging, and well-planned proposal. Your proposal is your business plan, your calling card, and your pitch as to why you are the right fit for a publisher. Knowing how crucial and exciting this opportunity may be, let's discuss the submission process to most major houses.

Creating the Proposal

Now that we have discussed the importance of creating a proposal, let's dive headfirst into the essential pieces of a quality proposal. Remember, this is an opportunity to sell you, your idea, and your platform to a prospective publishing house. You position your manuscript for success when it is well executed. Depending on the specific publishing house, they may require a particular format or sections to the proposal. So start by reviewing your receiver's expectations and preferences before beginning to work.

You will find more flexibility with the proposal's expectations assuming you are submitting through an agent or directly to a specific connection at any given house. Furthermore, a publisher may require less information and formality if you have published before. But assuming you are a first-time author or unfamiliar with the proposal process, we would strongly suggest you take the time to create an encompassing proposal with the following well thought out sections:

Cover-Page: The cover page is like the highlight reel for the manuscript. It should include the title of the book, the author's name, maybe even a sharp and representative photo of the cover or the author, and finally, a few bulleted highlights or selling points with which you would want to lead. Ultimately, this is your first impression and it should appear sharp, informative, and desirable. Using colors, keywords, and valuable selling points will only help to quickly engage a prospective publisher.

Snapshot of the Concept: Each and every book idea should have a unique selling point. This is the magic, the sparkle, or the differentiator. It separates your book from the others in any particular genre. Your snapshot should be hyper-focused and exciting. It should emphasize the foundation for the book and paint a beautiful picture regarding the topic and its viability. It is similar to a summary of the book, but with a whole lot more sizzle.

Proposal Contents: Publishers appreciate organization. Including a table of contents for your proposal offers that essential clarity. A thorough proposal can be between thirty and fifty pages, so a well-defined table of contents will allow publishers to effortlessly move to the most important parts of the proposal with ease. Consider creating a table of contents with hyperlinks that allow a publisher, with the click of his or her mouse, to move to the relevant part of the proposal. Remember, most publishers will review hundreds if not thousands of proposals over the course of the year. Saving them time so they can focus on the guts of your proposal will be much appreciated and beneficial to your project.

Market Research: Most books will fall into at least one, if not many, genres or markets. Publishers will both appreciate and benefit from extensive research and knowledge regarding the competition and richness of a category. They want to know if the market is saturated or growing; small or large, as well as the rate of success and sales of the market leaders. Amazon.com can provide a wealth of information regarding the market of a specific genre while providing a detailed summary of the trends and market leaders. Use market research to support your concept and demonstrate that your book will excel in an already flourishing genre.

Author Bio: Who are you? Why are you qualified to write this book? These are two of the first questions that will come out of any publisher's mouth. What separates you from every other mother out there that wants to write a book on parenting? Why are you different than every other life coach trying to write a self-help book? Your author bio section should celebrate your success and position you to be an expert on the subject matter. Don't be humble, but don't come across as unbelievable. Simply position yourself as an expert that will be able to tell the story and sell the book.

Promotion of the Book: Some people say this is the tail that wags the dog. For most publishing houses, promoting and marketing the book is just as important as the quality of the finished product. If you can't sell the book, they can't benefit from the deal. Consider each and every avenue you can to promote and market your book. Social media, philanthropic organizations, forthcoming speaking engagements, partnerships, interviews, media opportunities, endorsements, pre-sales, and all other forms of promotion should be included in this section. David Hancock, Founder and President of Morgan James reminds us that "the platform of a book is enormously important. Most publishing houses only really market the top 1% of their books. So it is extremely important that the Author has a well thought out plan and is willing to do the hard work to help book sales." Remember, this is your one and only opportunity to demonstrate to your publisher not only that you can sell books, but also that you have considered how you will accomplish this enormous responsibility.

Target Market: For whom are you writing this book? Is it geared towards twenty-something women right out of college? Or how about middle-aged men in the middle of a mid-life crisis? Whichever it may be, take the time to consider and outline your target market. Publishers appreciate knowing for whom the book is targeted. It allows them to better understand the opportunity, as well as determine if the market is one they would like to reach. This is often an easy question to answer, and certainly one that should be addressed.

Table of Contents for the Book: Every proposal should include a table of contents for the forthcoming book. Take the time to consider clever and engaging chapter titles that are catchy and representative of the underlying message of each chapter. These should offer your publishers and readers a glimpse into the topic while simultaneously piquing their curiosity to read on.

Chapter Summary: Perhaps one of the most important parts of any professional proposal, your chapter summary should include the chapter title along with a two to three paragraph summary of each chapter, highlighting the general and specific messages and goals each chapter will meet. Take the time to consider each chapter as its own little book that should stand on its own, but relate to the bigger picture. This is your time to excite a publisher and create momentum for the forthcoming book.

Contact Information: Simple but often forgotten. Provide publishers with detailed contact information and multiple ways to get in touch. Include your full name, address, direct phone number, and email address. If possible, choose a professional address like a business rather than your home address. Publishers want to feel comforted in the notion they are entering into a business relationships with a businessman. Remember, the small pieces are what will separate your proposal from that of the competition.

Sample Chapters: Each and every proposal should include at least one or two sample chapters. Once publishers makes it through your extensive and detailed proposal, they want to be dazzled by your writing abilities and thoughtful message. Here is your big opportunity to knock their socks off. We always recommend you choose two of the most exciting and enticing chapters to include. Take enormous care and pay attention to detail to ensure these chapters are not only dazzling, but also an enticing representation of the book to come. Not all publishers even make it this far into your proposal, but if they do, you should really take the time to excite them with your sample chapters. Make sure you edit them and ensure they are readable and clear. We'd hate to see you lose a book deal because of a sloppy sample chapter.

There is no exact science to proposals. But we are confident that the more detailed and informative the proposal, the better chance you'll have at acquiring a book deal. David Hancock of Morgan James told us, "A good book proposal gives a publisher a good idea about why the Author is writing the book and why the reader would want to read it. The goal is to really create something special that stands out. One of the most impressive ways to accomplish this is by including media in the proposal. Include a link or two that takes a publisher to a website or YouTube video about the Author or concept. That has really stood out in previous submissions and often separates that Author from the rest."

Look at your proposal as a business plan for a prospective investor. Consider what you would want to know before turning over your hard-earned money. Don't overwhelm publishers with information, but also don't underwhelm them.

The goal should be to strike a happy medium between what they need to know, and what will just be deemed as too much information. As Terry Whalin told us, "The biggest mistake in a book proposal is often it is missing a critical piece of information. It's been said the most difficult thing to proof read in a document is something that is not there. It's the same with proposals. Often the writer will be missing a critical bit of information such as the projected length of the project or they will not include a competition section. *Every book* competes so the writer should not contend there is no competition because the book idea is unique. It is not."

Following the equation set forth above will position you to provide your prospective publisher with an enormous amount of information to consider before making a buying decision. To further the process and help you along the way, you can also check out Rick's Book Publishing Wizard at www.bpwiz.biz.

Securing an Agent

One of the most important decisions you will make as an author is securing representation for both you and your book concept. Most authors tell us they see enormous value in working with a professional book agent. The network, the friendships, the knowledge of the industry, and the connections are all enormously valuable to both you and your future aspirations as an author.

The first is through a literary agent. Literary agents add an enormous amount of credibility and connections for first time authors. Without an agent, it is enormously difficult to break the seal and get through to the people that matter. They are like the captain of the ship, steering you in the direction of your goals. Most talented agents are hyper-connected and can place a quality proposal not only with the right house, but also with the decision makers at that particular house. They are familiar with the market and the demand. You'd be surprised to find out that certain publishers may be on the lookout for a very specific genre of book at any given time. Wiley may currently be looking for non-fiction self-help and not Autobiographies while McGraw Hill may be scouring the planet for a strong Biography but have little interest in a new self-help book.

A literary agent is going to be in constant communication with the market and its pulse, always thinking about where he can place a new proposal. Once accepted by an agent, he can begin the process of connecting your proposal with the best house. In most occasions, agents will submit your proposal to multiple competitors to ensure numerous opportunities to obtain a book deal. If you are lucky, it may even create enough interest to justify multiple offers. Literary agents will generally email or directly connect your proposal with a publisher's representative. This positions your proposal to rise to the top of the stack and most publishers will give credence and credibility to submissions via a literary agent. That simple connection may be worth its weight in gold.

Literary agents are talented at placing books. Through their network and knowledge, they can create a direct line of communication between both you and a potential publisher.

But not every author requires representation. Some authors submit their proposals directly to a prospective publisher. A direct submission may be the way to go because a potential author may not have the platform, connections, or even the desire to work with an agent. In the age of the Internet, many publishers maintain websites and social media chock full of helpful information. In fact, many of those houses will allow you to directly submit proposals or openly contact their representatives. They may outline a submission process or even offer details on preferred content and style of the proposal.

Finding the right literary agent may seem like an overwhelming experience. But the best place to start is by researching your competitors. Consider other successful books in your particular market. Head to a bookstore or to Amazon.com and peruse through the first few pages of each book. In those first few pages, you will find the author offering an expression of gratitude to his agent. Begin by making a list of those agents. You'll quickly find the names of the big players in your space that have experience in representing your book's subject matter.

Once you compile a list of a dozen or so agents, take the time to research them via the Internet. Most agents will have some Internet or website presence that will outline their bio, physical location, and often, preferred topics of representation. There are agents out there that only handle self-help and others that prefer fantasy or fiction. Ensure that the agent to which you are submitting focuses on the type of book you are writing.

Next, sculpt a cover letter or email introducing your concept, your background, and your platform. Attach your well-crafted proposal to your letter and then submit to each of your preferred agents. Remember, agents can also be inundated with submissions, so be patient and plan to follow up or check-in after two to three weeks. That gives your submitting agent time to review your project and determine if it will be a good fit.

In addition to using other published books as resources to locate potential representation, spend time searching the Internet to locate relevant agents for your book topic. We live in a world of accessible information and googling terms like "literary agent self-help" or "literary representation non-fiction" will generate hundreds of results and websites for those agents. You can then visit their websites and research which agents would be a good fit for you and your book. Consider their previous success, body of work, location, and whether or not they are currently accepting submissions. Most agents have contact information listed on their sites, welcoming the opportunity to connect with authors just like you.

Finally, one of the most direct and accessible ways to connect with literary agents is at large writing events like Author 101 (www.author101university.com) or Book Expo America (www.bookexpoamerica.com). These are fantastic events hosted in various cities that connect the big players in the writing world. You wouldn't be surprised to meet some of the most respected literary agents and publishers in the country at these events. Attend them with book proposal in hand and be prepared to make a pitch if given the opportunity. For example, Author 101 alone invites at least a dozen literary agents and it is not uncommon for even first-time authors to secure representation at these events.

The value of a well-respected literary agent cannot be understated. Agents bring both leverage and connections to you and your project. In the hyper-competitive book market, you'll need to get every leg up on the competition. And generally, the personal cost is low. Most agents charge a small upfront fee of just a few hundred dollars to cover the usual expenses like copies, postage, and travel to meet with potential publishing houses. They then work off of a contingent percentage of your book sales. Most agents charge around 15% of fees you earn—a small price to pay for the value they bring to the process. In fact, most agents will spend time with you reviewing your proposal and offering feedback before it is even submitted. This offers particular value to first-time authors.

Once the proposal is complete and ready for dissemination, agents will carefully consider their resources and connections in the industry, often choosing a number of publishing houses to which they submit your book proposal. It is not uncommon for an agent to do an initial round of submissions to the most coveted houses and, depending on the interest level, do a second or third round of submissions at a later time. This allows your agent to target the best fits without closing the doors of opportunity if your first submissions don't pan out. The real fun begins once the proposal is submitted.

Understanding the Process

Remember, most major publishing houses require a professionally created book proposal. We briefly discussed the writing process, but let's take just a little more time to focus on the submission part of the show. Remember, book proposals offer a glimpse into the concept and promotion/marketing plan for the forthcoming book. But what happens after you ship your proposal off to a publisher? Most houses receive submissions via one of two ways.

As mentioned above, the traditional manner of submission is through a literary agent. Agents bring enormous value and leverage to any potential author. However, in the day of self-publishing and many successful independent publishers, we are quickly finding that non-traditional routes of publishing are beginning to offer authors without agents an opportunity to find great success. If taking the dive without a literary agent, focus your time and energy on understanding the submission process, as well as your potential publisher's preferences. In fact, many of the self-publishing houses and hybrid publishers like Morgan James do not even require agents and accept author submitted proposals via their website or direct contact.

Once your proposal is submitted, most publishers will take a few weeks to review your business plan for the forthcoming book. They will consider your bio, the concept, the overall market appeal, their need for the subject matter, your social media and marketing platform, and your prior success (or failures) as an author.

In fact, one of the first steps publishing houses take is researching on BookScan, a data provider for the book industry that tracks points of sale and book history, to determine if you previously published any books and if so, how many copies were sold. As you can imagine, those numbers play a critical role in the decision-making process. In the publishing world, most publishers believe past performance predicts future results.

After reviewing the proposal, a publisher will make an initial determination if he feels your particular manuscript would be a good fit for the house. If you pass the first screen, a publisher will generally review the submission with the submission board. Depending on the size of the house, your potential publisher's submission board may consist of a number of representatives of the company like other editors or publishers, or even the President or Vice President in smaller houses.

The publisher will then pitch the board, offering a global view of both you and your idea. He will discuss in great detail the "buying decision," as well as the viability of the book and the positives and negatives of acquisition. After pitching the board, the submission board will offer feedback, discuss the book and the Author, and often vote on whether to make an offer or pass on the book. As you can imagine, most publishers receive thousands of annual submissions. Very few of these proposals actually make it to a pub board, and an even lower percentage of those proposals are made an offer.

However, an offer may be made for the lucky few that pass the extensive scrutiny and submission board. This offer will include a payment of some upfront money, along with a contingent payment of future money earned by the book. Some houses will consider counteroffers or even negotiate with you or your agent for a larger advance or higher royalties. But the movement is often not significant, especially for a first time author. It comes pretty close to a take it or leave it sort of deal.

An advance is a payment of money from the publisher to the author. It is generally an advance against future money earned from the book, but it is guaranteed and earned by the author upon execution of the contract and acceptance of the completed and final manuscript by the house. Thus, it is usually broken into two even payments. After the book is published and as it earns, the advance is returned to the publisher. Once the book earns out and the advance has been satisfied, the publisher begins to pay the author of the book a royalty, or a percentage of the net income generated from sales of the book.

Once an offer is made and accepted, most publishers will submit a standard contract for your review. It will encompass the major terms of the agreement, including how and when you will be paid, the required length of the book, and the due date for the completed manuscript. The contract will also focus on content ownership, which usually remains with the publishing house. Remember, if you are offered a contract from a publishing house, take the time to review it. If you do not feel as if you have the skillset to truly understand the language of the agreement, invest a small amount of money into a contract lawyer or seasoned literary agent to review the document and ensure it is a fair agreement. Ultimately, you have to abide by the document you sign.

Once the contract is executed, you will be in the exciting position to actually write the book. We will go into the writing process in more detail throughout the book, but make sure you pace yourself and remain organized because you are on the path to join a small group of people who are talented and successful enough to call themselves published authors.

But remember that it all starts with the proposal. Terry Whalin reminds us that while it is possible to obtain a book deal without a proposal, it can often be an uphill battle. He said, "It depends on who you want to publish your book. For a traditional publishing deal with a sizeable advance, you will need a well-crafted book proposal and a riveting sample chapter or chapters. Publishing is a consensus building process—particularly inside the larger publishing houses. That consensus happens when you find your champion inside the house and this champion is able to sell his colleagues on the merits of your project. It is hard to do that sort of internal consensus building without a complete book proposal."

Collectively, the goal is to create the best possible opportunity to secure a publishing deal. We firmly believe a well-crafted and complete proposal positions you to reach this lofty goal. Remember to take the time and thought to ensure your proposal is ultimately a representation of your best foot forward. Even the smallest mistake or victory can truly be the difference between reaching your objectives or not. Use your resources, lean on your valuable advisors, and don't settle for anything short of your greatest efforts.

Chapter 6

PLANNING AND OUTLINING

Everything has been said before, but since nobody listens
we have to keep going back and beginning all over again.
—Andre Gide

This chapter covers:
- Starting points
- Early research
- Noodling
- Book proposals
- Manuscripts
- Outlining

Starting Points

Many book projects never get off the ground because the writers don't know where to start. They spend so much time and energy agonizing over where to start that they become paralyzed and never begin. When they gather information, they can get lost in it, overwhelmed by it, or discouraged when they can't find the perfect starting point. Don't fall into these traps!

Frequently, writers can't get started because they don't have a plan on how to bring their books to life. So, now that you've sharpened your focus and zeroed in on what you want to write, the next step is to create a plan for how you will write your book. And that begins with the creation of a structure for your book, determining how you will present your book's content.

Barry Boyce, author of *The Mindfulness Revolution: Leading Psychologists, Scientists, Artists, and Meditation Teachers on the Power of Mindfulness in Daily Life* (Shambhala, 2011), offers his advice for a preferred attitude towards writing books. "You're better off than you think, because you've done this before, just not in as large a format. Almost every technique and skill you've used to structure and tell a story at feature length scales to book length. So, let go of the excess anxiety about never having done this before."

He continues by offering advice regarding structuring such a large format: "Planning. Planning. Planning. It's a campaign. I used some project management tools in the end to put some order into the vastness. That's the thing about the bigger scale. It requires more management to support the creativity. Cultivate a good relationship with your editor from the beginning. He/she is going to be your taskmaster at some point. That's going to go so much better if he/she is also your friend, colleague, supporter, and fan. The campaign of writing a book can get so lonely sometimes, you need a good "attaboy" just to remind yourself of why you're doing it and that you're not the crazy loser who needs to get out more."

When it comes to structure, you have many options. You can follow the format of most books by presenting information in a logical, narrative approach with a beginning, middle, and end. Or your book can tell a story, or it can state problems and give their solutions. Your book can be in the form of a list or series of lists, such as "10 Income Tax Saving Measures." Or it can cover a subject from A to Z or other divisions.

As we've mentioned, books are works in progress that constantly change. So the structure that you initially select can, and probably will, change. However, it's important to create an initial structure in order to give yourself a starting point, a place where you can begin to work on the book, even if that structure will subsequently change.

Robyn Says

Usually, it's more important to get going than to pinpoint the perfect starting point. Create a loosely knit structure or flexible road map for your book by listing your chapter areas and the main points you wish to address. Don't waste time organizing, revising, or refining every detail until after you've jumped in, since most books are works in progress that change. After you list your chapter headings, select a chapter to tackle first. I prefer to start at the beginning, with the introduction, and then move on to Chapter 1.

If it makes it any easier, think of your book's initial structure as a "working" or "temporary" format and expect it to change. Consider it a launching pad that will get you off the ground and expose you to materials that you can explore. Then take in all the information you find; be flexible and open to adjusting your plans.

"Be sure that this book will be different than what's out there or better," Florence M. Stone suggests. "Visualize the book; how many chapters, what each will be on and explain some of the substance of each chapter. This organizes your thinking and your focus."

"Focus is so important," David Fryxell points out. "Because everything you do in terms of research—reading, interviewing, gathering facts and information— really needs to be informed by that focus. A lot of people end up with mounds of research material, but then they can't write anything because so much of it doesn't pertain to their book's focus."

Early Research

After you've found your focus, it's usually necessary to conduct some initial research in order to get a clearer picture of what you want your book to be and to create a working structure for it. You also may need to obtain more information to write a book proposal. For example, you may need statistics on the size of the groups your book targets and the dollars they spend to address the problems your book covers. Or you may want to gather more background information on the seriousness of those problems, how they arose, and the unsuccessful methods that were used to try to fix them.

Before Theodore Kinni, coauthor of *No Substitute for Victory* (Prentice Hall, 2005), writes a book proposal, he tries to keep the up-front research to a minimum because at that point, you usually don't have a publishing contract and you're writing on speculation. Your agent and publishers are basically the major tests of whether your book idea is marketable. "If your agent doesn't like it or you can't find a publisher, it generally means that you don't have a marketable book idea," Kinni believes. "They can be wrong, they may miss the point or not be ready to move where you want them to go, but generally they have a good grasp of the market and what will sell."

"First, I do research to find out about the topic," Florence M. Stone says. "The most important thing is to find out how many books are out there. A visit to Amazon is always worthwhile, and I go to a local Barnes and Noble to see the book titles and find out if there's anything resembling what I have in mind. If books are being sold that are too close, it's not good. If they're somewhat related, but not exactly the same, you can still consider the idea."

Frequently, your preliminary research will dictate just how the book should be arranged and the information it should include. It may also clarify how you should begin, build, and finish or whether your book should be written in some other format.

Your initial research may merely require you to review the materials you've collected on the subject and stored in your files. Examine that information; see if you can organize it by placing it in order in your folders or files. Some writers, especially those who write research-heavy books, list each item in their files in a separate control file. Some have a computer control file or attach a printed listing to their hard-copy files or folders so they don't have to rummage through everything to find information they need.

The Internet is ideal for preliminary research. You can also conduct interviews and reread the notes you compiled when you examined comparable books. When you find information on the Internet that you might be able to use, print it out and place the hard copies in your folders or files.

Review the notes you took when you checked comparable books. For instance, you might have written down how your competitors structured their books, what information they included, how they set it forth, and what you would do differently. You also may have noticed how their books were designed, if they looked inviting or interesting, and how they felt in your hands. If you didn't, go back and carefully reexamine comparable books and take detailed notes. Don't copy their structure, however. Instead, use them as sources of inspiration for formats that could work for your book and be sure to list those elements you want to avoid.

- Make a list of the publishers whose books you like and who you think might be interested in your book.
- Give the publishers' names and the titles of the books that you liked to your agent.
- Identify publishers that you would prefer to avoid.

Don't risk leaving any of this information to your memory—write down what you like and dislike about each house.

When Louis Patler is intrigued by a book idea, he explores it, finds out who else is toying with it, and then looks into how it's being handled in practice. For example, if he wants to learn what's new with regard to corporate flextime or vacation policies, he reads up on the issues and then speaks directly with HR people and analysts. He then compares what he found with his own experience as a consultant for businesses. Patler focuses on the approaches that businesses are using, those that are working and the buzz about their practical implementation, not their abstract, theoretical side. He obtains two-thirds of the information included in his books through firsthand experience.

Katherine Ramsland is always collecting information that might work in the many book ideas she is considering. She places that information according to subject in piles or boxes. Ramsland told us that she has had one book idea for ten years and isn't sure that she will ever get to it. As of now, it hasn't taken the foreground as other books have. "Things always come up that are more timely or need to be quickly addressed," Ramsland states. "It's like triage; I give attention to whatever needs it right now."

All of Judy Ford's ideas and information for her books come from her experience, her clients, her friends, her life, and her thoughts. She doesn't talk to others about her books and doesn't read other books on subjects she may cover because she wants her writing to be "fresh from me." When she's writing, Ford may read material that touches and inspires her about writing. She also listens to spiritual or inspiring music because she believes it helps her creativity.

My Favorite Part

In his book projects, Joseph Cardillo enjoys the writing most, but he also finds it to be the most difficult part of the process. "When I'm writing, I feel better, it makes me feel content and complete as a person. And that feeling carries over into other parts of my life," Cardillo explains.

Noodling

For many authors, writing is simply an extension of who they are or what they do. They don't conduct much external research, but largely draw from within. Many have interesting ways to trigger their creativity.

A prime example is Dr. Brenda Shoshanna, author of *The Anger Diet* (Andrews McMeel Publishing, 2005) and six other books, two e-books, and dramatic plays. Dr. Shoshanna is a psychologist who has an active practice, teaches, and has given over five hundred workshops. She also reads constantly. So Dr. Shoshanna has accumulated a storehouse of information that she uses in her books.

When Dr. Shoshanna decides to write a book, she takes a notebook and goes to a park to be in nature. In her notebook, she writes different points, themes, ideas, memories, information, images, anecdotes, quotes, exercises, and whatever else comes to mind that could relate to the book. She calls her entries noodles because she's noodling around. Then she draws loops that connect her noodles together and indicates how they relate.

Dr. Shoshanna compares her noodling to the preliminary sketches artists draw before they begin to paint. "When I noodle, I never censor myself,"

Shoshanna reveals. "I just open the doors and let anything come out. And I try to free associate. As I noodle, everything seems exciting, innovative and even groundbreaking. So I let it sit to see if it will stand the test of time. After a few days, much of it may sound silly, but some will hold up; it's a weeding-out process."

Dr. Shoshanna uses her noodles as the basis for her book's chapters. She thinks about how she can cohesively capture the themes she would like to include. "I want to make the book a journey, so I try to structure the chapters to make it flow. I ask, 'What is point one and how does it lead to point two? What do I want readers to learn in Chapter 1? What do I want them to learn in Chapter 2? What understanding will they have when they've read the book?'"

After she noodles, Dr. Shoshanna decides on the book's title because "the title must capture what the book will be about." She opens a computer file and breaks down the book into chapters, gives each chapter a working title and lists what each will include in narrative sentences. She calls her process "building a bridge." When she gets into the actual writing, it's easy for her because she has done so much thinking and organizing that she's basically just filling in the blanks.

Book Proposals

"Unless you plan to self-publish, never write a book before you know that the book will sell to a publisher," Florence M. Stone declares. "Writing a book is a time-intensive chore. There will be times when you will be tired, have had a hard day, but you have a deadline with a number of pages to turn out. You must be sure that the book will be of interest to a book publisher. In fact, don't even start on a proposal until you know that there is interest in your book. Writers often have to change the middle of a book they've already been working on because a publisher may like the book idea, but not the approach or focus you took. I've come to the conclusion that if I can't write a proposal, I can't write the book."

"When you get a viable book idea, one that is strong enough for a book, the first thing you have to do is sell it," according to Al Ries, who coauthored *The Origin of Branding* (Harper Collins, 2004) with his daughter Laura Ries. "The world is awash in manuscripts. And many of them never get published. The most important thing is to sell the book first and then write it."

Author 101 Advice

"Proposals are also important because publishers like to feel that they're part of the process," according to Al Ries. "If they get a manuscript over the transom, they're not a part of the creation process and their instincts may be to reject it. When you give them a proposal, it allows them to put their imprint on it by saying what they like and what they don't. They get into the process and have a greater stake in it."

Writing book proposals can be extremely difficult work, but it beats writing an entire manuscript that publishers will not buy. Writers constantly complain about having to write proposals, and many consider it the most difficult part of writing a book. However, they tend to agree that it's ultimately beneficial to them because it makes them clarify exactly what the book will be about and what it will contain. If a publisher agrees to acquire a proposed book, the proposal gives writers a blueprint they can follow to complete the book.

Judy Ford takes a different approach. She works on the proposal at the same time she writes the book. Usually, Ford submits the proposal when about half of the book has been completed. By writing the proposal as she writes the book, she gets "a clear concept of what the book is. Then you can sell it well in your proposal."

As we stated in Chapter 1, publishers usually want book proposals that include certain information: an overview of the book, the author's biography, analysis of comparable books, the table of contents, chapter summaries, a promotion plan, and sample chapters. And to deliver much of this information, writers frequently must conduct some initial research.

Despite the fact that he's authored or coauthored nearly forty books, Jay Conrad Levinson still has to go through the proposal process, which he now appreciates because it forces him to develop the details of his books. Much of the material included in a book proposal can be used to write the book. For example:

- Portions of the overview that describe the book and its format could work well in the book's introduction or opening chapter.

- The chapter summaries are invaluable because they outline the content each chapter will contain.
- The analysis of comparable books helps authors identify their niche and sharpen their focus.
- Authors can frequently import their tables of contents and sample chapters directly into their books with little or no change.

Florence M. Stone finds that writing the overview (introduction) is the most difficult part of the proposal. She starts by preparing a rough draft that says, "'the purpose of this book is.' Then, I try to explain the benefits that readers will get by buying this book. If I can't do that, there is no point in going any further with the proposal."

"Then in two or three paragraphs I explain what this book is going to do and how it's going to be different from all the other books out there," Stone continues. "After I've identified those benefits, I can write them up in a more polished and developed version. However, I need to know and state in the proposal a number of reasons why readers will buy and read this book."

"Writing the table of contents and sample chapter is very difficult because you haven't done the heavy research yet," Charles Cerami states. "You have to do some research to show how knowledgeable you are about the material, but for a proposal, you don't want to conduct extensive research for a book that a publisher may not want." Unfortunately, it's a necessary part of the process that, at the least, takes him several weeks.

When writers draft book proposals, they usually send them to their agents. If they don't have agents, they should send query letters to editors or agents who might be interested in their books.

When Charles Cerami puts together a formal book proposal, he sends it to his agent, Bob Silverstein. Silverstein will often find items that need improvement or change, so Cerami makes the necessary changes and, after a time or two, the revised proposal is usually acceptable to Silverstein, who will then submit Cerami's proposal to eight or ten publishers.

After the contract is signed, Cerami works from the proposal, which "instructs me as to how I should go ahead. Then I go into libraries and conduct the research I need to develop the content. I look for diaries and memoirs that have individuals' own words. Then I write down whatever catches my eye in no particular order, just as I come across them."

When Katherine Ramsland gets a book idea, she reads to get background information. Since she knows that she will have to write a book proposal to sell the book, she thinks in terms of the proposal as she researches. She constantly asks:

- How will the proposal be laid out?
- What will the overview be?
- How will I write the concept statement and the outline?
- What sample chapters should I include?

After Ramsland collects information on her book ideas and before she starts writing the proposal, she takes a long walk, which helps the proposal fall into place. She also sleeps on it. Ramsland writes the proposal as much for herself as for publishers because it organizes the information and makes clear to her what she really knows about the subject, what her weaknesses are, what she needs to fill in, and what experts she needs to help her and how she will reach them. Before she writes a proposal, Ramsland conducts extensive research. She has spent as much as a year working on a proposal, but then again, she has written others in a day.

Ramsland's agent helps in the process by suggesting changes and revisions, which she usually makes. She trusts her agent greatly because he knows the market and suggests titles that interest her.

Robyn keeps a master book file, which she backs up. When she opens a master file, she also begins building the proposal for that book. Since Robyn is always working on a few books at once, her master files help her stay organized and capture her interests. Robyn has let some of her book ideas sit for years before she wrote proposals for them.

My Least Favorite Part

Stephen Yafa dreads writing book proposals. "Having to write a proposal makes me feel like I'm back at school and I have to finish some awful assignment. It makes me think about the book more deeply than I'm usually ready for," Yafa bemoans. "But it also forces me to map out the book in detail and see what I've got. And, when I'm ready to write, it really helps me because I've got a great outline to follow."

Manuscripts

If you decide not to go the proposal route, as so many self-published authors do, you will have to write a complete manuscript. Since you won't have a table of contents, you will have to build it from scratch. In addition, you won't have chapter summaries, which outline the content of each chapter. So, to lay out your book and identify your needs, you will probably have to conduct preliminary research.

One of the major difficulties in writing a manuscript is that it's often a big, daunting task that requires planning and organization. Many books are information intensive, so they can be overwhelming and cause writers to go off course. To avoid such pitfalls, break your work into smaller, more achievable chunks that you can attack one by one. Completing individual portions will be encouraging and can build your confidence and resolve. And the list of the pieces you tackle can help you write your table of contents, the road map for your book.

Richard Narramore, Senior Editor at John Wiley & Sons discusses the value of a riveting table of contents. He says, "The table of contents is a key marketing piece of any book. Chapter titles should make browsing readers on the fence want to buy the book. Look at your table of contents as an opportunity to draw your readers in. Consider it from the perspective of a copyrighter. Try to write chapter titles that can stand-alone and push a reader to purchase the book. Deliberately choose chapter titles that attract people. Then, add a more explanatory subtitle that tells readers what the chapter is about. Especially with non-fiction books, readers are less likely to read books cover to cover. So, a well-executed table of contents allows readers to jump around. The book may be worth the price for just one or two chapters and the table of contents should signal to the reader that these one or two chapters are there."

- Don't worry about finding the perfect chapter titles.
- Concentrate on identifying the material that you want to cover.
- Determine the order that the material you will cover should follow.
- Break down the book into chapters.
- List the content that will be included in each chapter.
- Note what additional information you will need.

Create a research plan for the information you need. First, list the materials you need and where you think you can find them. For example, if you believe that you can get certain information in books or articles, identify where you can locate the reading material you want. If you need to conduct interviews, decide whom you want to interview and how to reach them. Creating a research plan will begin to condition you to incorporate more planning and forethought in the writing of your book, an understanding that many writers receive when they write book proposals.

Research plans provide orderly steps for you to follow: they tell you what to do first, second, and so on. They help you incrementally collect and build a body of information that you can integrate into your book and to identify the gaps that you should fill.

How you proceed to write about the information you obtain through your research is strictly up to you. You have a number of options: some authors write while they gather information; others wait until they've compiled a substantial amount of information before they start to write; and still others find a happy medium by gathering some information, writing, and then conducting more research to fill in any holes.

Rick Says

Adopt one system for writing up your research discoveries and stick with it. If the first method you chose works, continue using it. If it doesn't, then try other ways. But once you find a system that works, keep using it. Using different systems over the course of a book project can be confusing and can undercut your organizational efforts.

Outlining

Outlining is the step most writers take after they conduct their preliminary research, but before they try to actually write their books. Many writers create their outlines from the table of contents and chapter summaries that they submitted with their book proposals.

The word *outline* gives chills to many would-be authors; it makes them recall those hateful diagrams they were forced to construct in school. Well, forget about those formal outlines; don't worry about alternating numbers, letters, and their various forms. Instead, think in terms of lists that will identify the information that should go in your book and the order in which it should go.

- Keep your outlines simple and don't worry about their form.
- Include enough words or entries to create a working plan.
- After you list your entries, expand on them by adding additional ideas and information.
- Review your outline frequently and keep adding to it. The more detail you provide, the easier it will be when you write.

Katherine Ramsland makes a computer file for each of the chapters that she created for her book proposals. Then she uses the chapter summaries as outlines for the chapters and expands on them. At that time, she decides if she still wants to keep the chapters in the same order in which they were listed in the proposal. Often, she will change them because of new developments that may have occurred.

Mary Roach's outlines evolve. She usually starts with the rough versions that she submitted with her book proposals. Then she transfers the information, in pencil, to blank paper that she posts on her wall. This allows her to glance up while she works to get a sense of where she is and where she has to go. If she's stalled on a chapter, she can quickly see other chapters she may want to tackle.

Roach's outlines are very rough; they are informal and change constantly. They don't have roman numerals or capital letters. After a few months, her book outline generally gels and she sticks to it with a few minor variations. By the time she really gets into the writing, Roach usually has a solid outline that lists which chapters go where. Her outlines contain only the order of the chapters and don't detail the content included in each.

Although David Fryxell does everything else on the computer, he writes his outlines by hand. Working by hand lets him draw arrows, indicate inserts, cross things out, and color different entries to indicate their importance and/or priority.

Fryxell creates his outlines on a yellow legal pad. Since they are extremely detailed and complete, his outlines don't tend to evolve much. Interestingly, a number of writers told us that they compose their outlines by hand, not on the computer, and that they use yellow legal pads.

In his writing, Fryxell occasionally strays from his outline. For instance, he may wander when he finds connections, transitions, or levels of detail that previously had not occurred to him, or information that would work better in other places. He will cut a section that is running long, an item that has been fully covered, repetitious content, or material that doesn't really fit. However, since his outlining is so detailed, he rarely adds new ideas or different takes on old ideas.

Although Malcolm Gladwell makes loose outlines, he doesn't stick to them, "because you can't. It changes," Gladwell observes. "I just make outlines because I have ideas and I want to make sure that I have a record of them. But I don't really have a formal outline that I follow."

When he was younger, Gladwell outlined more. Now that he's a more experienced writer, he outlines intuitively, subconsciously, in his head, but not formally on paper or the computer. He feels that he has developed a sense of where he's going, and that's usually good enough.

Stedman Graham puts the information that he finds in his preliminary research into folders. When he feels he has enough information to map out a book, he takes the folders and outlines the information in them. He concentrates on being "current with the way the industry is going and including information that's relevant to the marketplace." Graham outlines both by hand and on the computer. He outlines primarily by hand because it helps him generate ideas. As the conceptual or starter person on his book projects, he tries to kick-start ideas and flesh them out, but he doesn't do much of the detailed research. Graham's main role is to come up with ideas, ignite those ideas, give them to his staff, and get his staff to begin to organize a program around them. Then his staff conducts whatever research is needed.

Brad Schoenfeld outlines each of his books in great detail. He visualizes each chapter and the material it should contain. Then he tries to write the outline as fully as possible, which helps him to write the book. Schoenfeld doesn't necessarily work in a linear chapter-to-chapter manner, but he writes about whatever inspires him and then goes back in and fills in the gaps.

Speculation Pie

Arthur H. Bell creates what he calls a speculation pie. He feels that he is relatively disorganized, so he doesn't create a rigid A, B, C outline before beginning to work. However, he needs to see the whole canvas, so he draws what he calls a speculation pie: a circle divided by lines that resemble slices or wedges. In the slices, he writes whatever comes to mind and he doesn't overly censor himself. Bell's objective is to list points that he can cover, and he knows that all those items may not work.

Since Bell teaches and consults on the subjects of his books, he is usually able to quickly fill in about 80 percent of each slice. Although the remaining portions are not as clear, they usually emerge as he works through the book. He feels that 20 percent often gives rise to his best ideas, items he would not have originally considered. Bell believes that your last ideas, those that are forced out, can become some of your best ideas, and some of your first ideas, which are most obvious, may ultimately not be usable.

From his speculation pie, Bell begins structuring the book into ten to twelve chapters. He usually tries to design the first chapters to give the reader a picture of the entire journey because he thinks readers need to know what they're getting into. Chapter one usually paints that picture, and the next two or so chapters describe the problems that the book will solve.

"Take your time, don't rush into theories or solutions, but state the problems that you think readers face," Bell cautions. "When readers are brought along this way, they feel that the writer understands them and their problem, which makes them more willing to put in the time and effort it takes to read the book." In the first 20–25 percent of the book, Bell likes to carefully describe and analyze the problems. "Then the rest of the book unfolds naturally because both you and the reader know the piece you've bitten off to chew and the expectation is that the rest of the book will go into practical solutions for the different dimensions of the problems," Bell declares.

Two Outlines

After Jay Conrad Levinson conducts his initial research, he spends an hour or so outlining the book. He actually makes two outlines. For the first, he writes a sentence on each chapter in order to describe it and explain what it will contain. Since he's gathered so much research, which he's organized internally, he can write these descriptions quickly; they seldom take him more than a half hour to an hour to complete. He uses one sheet of paper and the initial outline is usually handwritten.

After he completes the first outline, he lets it sit for a few days; he reflects on it and allows it to sink in. Then he reviews it and makes changes that might be necessary. At this point, Levinson is interested in creating a logical flow of information. When he writes the second outline, he writes one page on each chapter and includes the information that he is going to cover in that chapter. This outline he submits with his book proposals, and he finds it to be essential when he actually begins to write the book because he now has detailed instructions on everything that should be included in each chapter.

"I now realize that I'm not writing my chapter summaries for the publisher," Levinson confesses, "I'm doing it for myself because it's really my detailed road map for the book." It also gives him the opportunity to spot what may be missing, things that should be checked, and what could be expanded to strengthen the book. Levinson then may make notes to himself to fill in those blanks or answers, or he can stop to fill in whatever is needed on the spot. Since it's so easy to get information via the Internet, Levinson usually does it immediately. "I'll take a detour from my writing in order to do more research to take care of the loose ends that I find as I go along. And because the process of writing a book is so long, lots of things can happen that I may want to get in," Levinson notes. "When I'm writing, I don't stop my life. I still read, research and try to learn. If, in midbook, I find something I should include, I stop, research it, and add it." That keeps his writing fresh and up to date.

During the time he completes the chapter summaries and the time he actually starts writing the chapter text, Levinson may add notes or references by hand that he would like to check or include. He also includes notes that may spur his thoughts.

Problem with Outlining

Al Ries is wary of outlines. "A book written through an outline is very jerky," he believes. "It has a headline and then something under it. Then it has a subheadline and something under it. It keeps going back and forth and doesn't flow. Writing a book should be like writing a play. Everything should build on what happened before. Chapter outlines don't work because you want your chapters to be more like conversations where you talk about related subjects and then go onto something else in another chapter. So it's important to get a cohesive flow, rather than to just blurt out things."

"When business books are written from an outline, the outline may make sense, but when authors write the book, they don't get the various points on the outline to flow together," Ries notes. "As a result, the reader gets lost. If the book flows, the reader will want to keep reading to find out what's next, what happened here, did this work or not and are there some exceptions to what you said. The only break that you should take is when you move from chapter to chapter, and even there, you should try to hook your chapters together, but sometimes it's impossible."

Action Items

1. Describe the type of preliminary research you may have to conduct.
2. Write ten noodles for your book idea.
3. Explain where outlining fits in the book-writing process.
4. State the main advantage of a detailed book outline.
5. Create a speculation pie for your book.

·················· **REMEMBER** ··················

Create a structure for your book and find a starting point. A starting point is critical, and many book projects are not completed because writers don't know where to begin. Work from the table of contents and chapter summaries that you submitted as part of your book proposal, or write them from scratch.

Although writing book proposals can be difficult, they help writers by forcing them to focus on, and more clearly define, their books. Much of the information submitted in proposals can also be used in writing the book. Book proposals give publishers the opportunity to have more input in shaping the book, which may make them more receptive to acquiring a property.

Chapter 7

RESEARCH

Get your facts first, and then you can distort them as much as you please.
—Mark Twain

This chapter covers:
- Continual research
- The Internet
- Interviews
- Surveys
- Case histories
- Documentation

Research is an essential part in writing virtually all nonfiction books and should be planned when possible. Even if you're writing a memoir, research is necessary in order to round out, fill in, or back up what you remember or may not know.

David Fryxell believes that you should, "Come up with a research plan. Decide where you want to go, what the most important things to look for are, where you will be most likely to find them. The two main questions are how will you do your research and how does it fit with the focus of your book so that you can eventually write it?"

Keep notebooks, Fryxell advises. Copy the research materials you find by hand into the notebooks because "when it goes through your arm to the paper, it tends to also put it in your brain," Fryxell believes. Copying information makes a deeper impression on you, and you may think about it more and remember it better. If you just photocopy pages, you can amass a mountain of paper that may be hard to organize and use, and you might not remember why you copied it in the first place.

When Katherine Ramsland gets the green light on a book from a publisher, she tries to figure out what she has to achieve to deliver the book by its deadline. Then she maps out what she must accomplish each week from the present time until the date the book is due. She simultaneously writes a combination research and writing plan, in which she determines which experts she needs to interview and estimates how many words she has to write each week.

It doesn't matter to Ramsland whether she will actually write a certain amount each week or interview a set number of experts. Her main concern is having the knowledge that she has a plan in place because it makes her feel organized and ready to go. A plan pulls her into the project and gives her a sense of momentum. Then she is able to get right in and work.

"People who start writing before they've conducted all of their research, usually write themselves into trouble," Al Ries observes. "You can write an article out of your head, but you can't write a book out of your head. You need tangible material before you start, so gather lots of tangible material." That material shows you what you have to write. When you start writing, you may spot holes that you need to fill in later. "It's essential to have collected the materials," Ries explains, "because it's easy to state principles. However, it's much harder to provide the information, case histories and examples that convince readers that the principles are correct."

Continual Research

In Chapter 2, we stated that reading is the best foundation for writing. Reading not only teaches writers about writing, but also provides them with many of their strongest book ideas. Successful writers tend to be great readers; many of them border on being obsessive readers, reading everything in sight.

Jay Conrad Levinson can't start his day without reading; reading is a major and constant part of his life. When Levinson reads, he's always looking for ideas and information that he could include in his books. "I don't consider it research," Levinson says, "although it really is, because it's such a central part of my life. It's a product of my natural curiosity and I think that I'd continually read and look for ideas even if I didn't write."

Gregory Godek reads constantly; it's his primary source of information. Each weekday, he gets five newspapers. He also subscribes to three Sunday papers and over fifty magazines. Godek immerses himself in information, and he has a detailed system for keeping track of it.

Godek doesn't read everything he receives, but he scans it all. As he scans, he rips articles out and saves whatever looks interesting. Godek considers himself "relatively indiscriminate," so he rips and saves a great deal; anything he feels he might possibly want or need. Godek works his way through every page of the daily papers and the Sunday *New York Times*.

Godek may rip out as many as forty articles from a Sunday newspaper. He prioritizes the articles he saves, putting them in one of four boxes: (1) material he wants to read that day, (2) items he should read soon, (3) possible background articles, and (4) other information that he might want to read someday. Godek regularly works through his four piles; it's a constant process that never stops.

When he goes grocery shopping, Godek will grab a handful of articles from the top of his "read now" file and go over them while he waits in line. Constantly reading and obtaining information, Godek finds, inspires and energizes him and his ideas.

As Godek reads articles, he highlights and enters notations on them. When an article contains a great phrase, idea, quote, or fact, he marks it and often adds an explanatory note. Then, if he doesn't look at it again for two years, the highlighted portion will catch his eye and the note may give it context. When he subsequently comes across the piece, he can just scan it and not have to wade through all of it to find what originally intrigued him.

Godek saves facts and statistics that could be helpful in the future. Leafing through his miscellaneous piles creates its own synergy for him, because as he scans, he stumbles upon ideas and information that could fit into or enhance many areas of his life and work. "It nourishes my creativity and gives my mind new places to go," Godek states.

When Godek finds a piece of information that is directly related to what he is writing or developing, he will enter it into a computer file. Usually, just entering it will spark an idea, so he will write a paragraph or two about it. He usually references the source, for example, "the *New Yorker* magazine, March 22, 2002, p. 31." Otherwise, he just leaves it to his memory.

Stedman Graham's research process starts with an Internet search on his particular interest. He looks for materials on the topic, such as books and articles. Graham is also a committed reader; he reads five or six business newspapers every day and looks for articles that impact subjects that he might write about or want to know more about for his business.

When Graham finds articles he could use, he prints or tears them out and files them in folders that he creates for the various projects on which he's working. Graham usually has many projects under way and developing them can take years. So, over time, he amasses a substantial amount of information on different subjects. When he feels that he has enough information on a topic to begin creating a book, he reviews the information in his files and outlines the materials he gathered. Graham's outlines become the structure for his books, and from there, he creates proposals for the titles he wants to write.

Graham's staff, friends, colleagues, and business associates know that he's always working on books, so they keep up to date on his areas of interest. They feed him information and leads that he might be able to use. Graham does not interview or conduct surveys; however, he will rely on other people's surveys. "There's a lot of information out there already in the education business. For us there's so much information out there, and we have to be concerned with being overwhelmed with information because it can cause you to lose your focus easily."

For *New York Times* Best-Selling Author Mitch Albom, his research comes from listening to others. He says, "I tell stories. For a while I told stories through music and then I told stories in newspapers and later I told stories in books, the best-known being *Tuesdays with Morrie*, a story about my old teacher who was living to the fullest even as he was dying. But before I started telling stories, I heard them. My family loved to rattle them off, especially the senior members, grandparents and uncles and aunts, usually around a Thanksgiving table, always with plates of food close at hand. These were stories about family, history, war; some might have even been closer to fairy tales. Someone would inevitably say, "Oh, no, not THAT one again," but we would settle in and listen anyhow. I never minded. In fact, I loved it. Those stories made me feel part of something, gave me stories of my own, as if my elders' tales, through their telling, could become my tales, too."

When Dan Baker begins a book project, he reads extensively to become more informed. He then reviews his personal contacts to see whom he could recruit to help. For his upcoming book, *What's Right with America's Corporations* (Rodale, 2006), Baker enlisted Dr. Cathy Greenberg and Collins Hemingway as coauthors. He put out the word about the project with guests at his place of employment, and they directed him to others, whom he interviewed and asked for leads. Basically, he knocked on doors, spoke with experts, and got leads and referrals.

"Anyone thinking about writing would be well advised to get on the Internet, go to the library and figure out what's out there," Baker suggests.

Many authors keep separate files for quotations, statistics, facts, and other information that they might use. They will regularly cut out and file items that could be of interest down the road. Then, as they write their books, they will review these files and use whatever might help.

The Internet

Research information is now easier thanks to the Internet. With a few clicks, you can get lists of articles, books, and other information on your specific interest. You can identify books published about your interest and when they were published and by whom. Frequently, you can see their cover images and read their tables of contents, descriptions, and reviews. You may also be able to read selected chapters or excerpts. From the Internet, you can begin to develop an overall understanding of your topic and learn about directions that you may want to pursue.

Although the Internet can help you get started, it also can flood you with information, much of which can be totally irrelevant. So you have to carefully sift through entries and check them for additional leads. And although the process can be tiring, it's often better than sitting for hours in drafty libraries and searching through dusty books.

"When you Google anything," Greg Godek observes, "it doesn't give you any synergy. You'll get stuff by your competitors and what's in the media, but by the time anything gets in the media, it's not leading edge anymore. Even the most techie magazines are a couple of months behind. And the best new ideas are usually going to come from outside your industry, where focused searches like Google searches don't take you. Essentially, Google keeps you confined in your own particular area according to the search and classification parameters they've set. So you'll miss some great opportunities."

Avoid that danger by reading broader sources of information such as newspapers and *Time*, *Newsweek*, and *Forbes* magazines, Godek suggests. "Get all of the other stuff that's going on because we're living in a world of context in which many things connect. When you read, watch, and hear from a wide scope of sources, you get new information and ideas that you get to filter to see how it jibes with your own interests. Even if you have the best filter and are the top expert, you still need information that can tie you into new ideas and directions."

Google searches are great for secondary research. They help you find and focus on items and areas of interest. However, they are not replacements for broader investigations that introduce you to new ideas. "People get mesmerized by technology, but it can be limiting—so they should check what else is around," Godek suggests.

Carl Zimmer, award-winning author of multiple books on animals and evolution agrees with this notion. He says, "Do as much research as possible away from the Internet—with living people, in real places."

My Favorite Part

Jeff Greenwald likes writing dialogue, researching, and meeting people best. He loves talking to them and hearing their stories. "I really enjoy writing once I'm into it, its rhythm, and I've established my voice," Greenwald tells us. "It's fun to plow through chapters, creating interesting turns of phrases and new ways of describing things. It's very rewarding to make something that's normally obscure or even unknown clear to people and I really enjoy that a lot."

Interviews

Interviews can produce a quality of information that may be difficult or impossible to otherwise obtain. When you interview experts, they can generally give you in just minutes information that may have taken them years or decades to acquire. They usually have amazing insights and can connect items in their fields to broader issues and more universal and important themes.

Experts' knowledge and understanding are usually practical, not theoretical, speculative, or abstract. Their knowledge and understanding are based on their own hands-on experience. Experts can usually explain complex subjects clearly so that they're logical and easy to follow and understand. Experts know the pressing problems in their fields and usually have solved them—numerous times.

Quotations from experts can add color to your explanations. Their stories and observations can cut straight to the point and clarify and demystify the muddiest matters. Experts also tend to know and be involved with other experts. So they can refer you to the top practitioners in their related fields. These referrals can bring you new information streams that can make your book fresh and exciting.

"It's like being an ambassador of goodwill," Robyn observes. "When I put the spotlight on people I interview, they give me amazing information. They are so proud to be featured in a book, and feel validated. A beautiful synergy evolves from sharing poignant stories and people inspire people."

Interviewing experts is usually fun because people love to talk about what they do well and feel passionate about. When they explain it to you, they can convey their passion and excitement. And when they sense that they're getting through to you, there is often no holding them back. They get expansive and come up with marvelous stories and anecdotes.

When you interview experts, they can breathe life and excitement into tasks and procedures that never before were of interest to you. It's both stimulating and fascinating because they can take you into their special world, give you the grand tour, and focus entirely on communicating with you. It makes you feel privileged, as if you've been invited to a magical place or let in on a fascinating secret. When you conduct interviews, get your subjects' permission to include their quotes.

Rick Says

Most of the information in this book was obtained through interviews and boy, were they fun. We made it a point to speak with top professionals, writers who have written numerous books and developed systematic approaches to their work. Speaking with them about our shared experiences, items that we also do, was exhilarating. Our interviews turned into conversations between peers, fellow writers who enjoyed talking about what we do.

What made our interviews for this book unusually special is that writers frequently talk about and explain the content of their books: their book ideas, themes, and the information they provide. But they rarely speak about their writing processes, their art. So we got to talk about the nuts and bolts of jobs like conducting research, organizing it, outlining books, writing, and editing, which we rarely get to talk about.

For *What's Right with America's Corporations* (Rodale, 2006), Dan Baker and his coauthors interviewed people face-to-face, by phone, and via e-mail. They recorded the interviews because "everything is fast paced and it's not easy to get it all down."

When you record interviews, it enables you to hold conversations rather than merely submitting questions. You can listen to the answers and don't have to worry about writing them down. As you're getting answers to your questions, you can drill down to get more specific responses or to move on to other points.

Tapes of interviews provide historical records that support the material you write. While you are interviewing someone, you may not grasp all the implications involved in what they said. However, when you subsequently listen to the tape and know more about the subject, you may hear important information that you initially missed or did not fully understand. If you wish, you can go back, follow up, and clarify matters that still may not be completely clear.

Frequently, people that you interview will send you books, articles, or other material that they've published. They may also give you their permission to quote their writing because it can give them good publicity.

Casey Hawley, author of *203 Ways to Turn Any Employee Into a Star Player* (McGraw-Hill, 2004), feels that interviews produce the best information. However, she points out that the information obtained can be difficult to organize and work into book form.

The bulk of Malcolm Gladwell's research, 90–95 percent, comes after the proposal stage. "In the proposal, you give them a flavor of what you're interested in, and after the proposal has been accepted, you fill things in," Gladwell reports. "You find stories, characters and people; you research ideas; and you do all kinds of things to fill it out." To get information, Gladwell conducts many interviews. He goes to see people and tries to get them to tell stories.

People are rich in stories, and stories make wonderful contributions to books. In our culture, learning is based on storytelling and has been for thousands of years. Storytelling personalizes lessons, makes them more graphic and easily understood and retained.

Daylle Deanna Schwartz, author of *How to Please a Woman in and out of Bed, 2nd Edition* (Adams Media, 2005), interviews extensively for her books. She mails interview questions to her subjects, posts them on her website (*www.daylle. com*), and brings them with her to speaking engagements. She also publishes two newsletters that always include requests to interview subjects.

"I could just talk from my point of view," Schwartz states, "but I'm not every woman. Readers relate to the people I've interviewed because they are real people who tend to have similar problems and feelings. They say, 'Wow, I'm not the only one who feels like that,' which makes a stronger impression than if I tell them to do or not do something or even that I also feel the same way."

Schwartz warns her subjects not to disclose to her anything that they don't want in print. A large percentage of her interviews are via e-mail, so respondents have time to think about their answers. As a result, they usually don't have regrets regarding how they responded.

The interview questions that Schwartz asks are pointed; they delve and involve deep-rooted feelings. For example, she will ask, "How did you feel when you said yes all the time to people, when you really wanted to say no?" "How did you feel when you looked in the mirror when other people told you that you were attractive and you didn't feel attractive?" "What were you seeing that you felt they didn't see or what do you feel they didn't see?"

Since Schwartz relies heavily on interviews, she often sends subjects what she calls "first level questions," which are preliminary or opening questions to learn where they are and about their problems, interests, and objectives. Then, she will follow them with secondary questions that focus more sharply on the information initially revealed.

Schwartz will also send out long lists of questions and request that the recipients answer only those in which they're most interested. She asks that her questions be answered in full sentences that run no longer than a single paragraph. Questions can be skipped. When she receives answers, she works them into the materials she writes.

David Finkel explained the enormous amount of time he spent interviewing and researching returned soldiers for his Best-Selling book, *Thank You for Your Service* (Sarah Crichton Books, 2013). "The short answer is a year and a half, but the more accurate answer is ever since early 2007. I say that because my research really started when I embedded with the 2-16 infantry battalion during its fifteen-month deployment to eastern Baghdad during the Iraq War 'surge' of 2007-2008. The story of what happened to those soldiers became my first book, *The Good Soldiers*, and *The Good Soldiers* is what allowed and informed *Thank You For Your Service*, which is the second volume of the story. In Iraq, I was with Adam Schumann on the day he so guiltily left the war, and Tausolo Aieti on the day he was blown up and his dreams began. I met Nic DeNinno there and was there on the day that James Doster died. After *The Good Soldiers* was published in 2009, it became clear that the story was only partly told. So many of the soldiers, home now, and so many of their families, were tipping over so many edges. Their war had become an after-war, and so I began traveling to Kansas, where the 2-16 is based, to see what I might be able to write. That brings me back to the short answer of eighteen months, which was how long I spent with the Schumanns, the Aietis, the DeNinnos, the surviving family of James Doster, and the rest of the people documented in *Thank You For Your Service*. That's how long it took for me to feel confident that the story I'd be writing would feel true to a reader and true to them as well."

Surveys

Although surveys are not usually as sharply focused as interviews, they can produce a wider range of valuable information. In interviews that are conducted in person or by phone, the interviewer can drill down and ask pointed follow-up questions that can produce more precise and/or in-depth information. An interviewer can latch onto a particular line of questioning and learn about it in great detail. A skilled interviewer will also sense a subject's feelings and when other lines of inquiry could be fruitful, and quickly shift gears to move the conversation in those directions.

Since surveys are composed of lists of written questions, they may not be as productive or as flexible as personal or telephone interviews. Usually, they don't go into the depth of more focused interviews, are not as fully answered, and can be difficult to clarify and follow up. Frequently, people will not answer long lists of survey questions, so they are usually more productive when they're brief.

On the plus side, surveys can be invaluable tools for obtaining wide consensus on issues, directions, and trends. In one survey, a surveyor can obtain a strong indication of how a representative sampling of individuals feel and what they want, like, and dislike.

Robyn Says

A survey can validate ideas or information on which your book is based. If you ask only a limited number of questions, the cost and work involved in conducting a survey can be relatively low. Test your questions beforehand to make sure that they're clear and provide the type of information you seek. Consider asking open-ended questions that people can fill in.

If you plan to hire a firm to conduct your survey, interview a few and get references. Review examples of surveys they've run for others. Compare costs, methods, and time frames. Find out how all results will be documented and what documentation you will receive. Request that you be given results in a summarized fashion that you can use in your book.

To identify the mistakes that women felt they made in dealing with money for her book *Nice Girls Don't Get Rich*, Lois P. Frankel sent an email to everyone in her network—hundreds of women. But she found that the basic premise she asked about, that women get different messages about money than men do, was wrong. Women and men get the same basic messages—save for a rainy day, be financially independent, and spend within your means. So, she concluded that she asked the wrong question.

Frankel then sent a second e-mail, asking women what mistakes they had made that precluded them, at this stage of their lives, from having the amount of money they needed to live how they wished. From the answers, it was clear that although men and women get the same messages, women get double messages. After they are taught the same basic principles as men about handling money, they are told, "Well, you really don't need to go to graduate school because you'll only end up getting married." Effectively, many of the messages women received were subsequently taken away. The responses Frankel received helped her sharpen and better her original ideas.

Frankel categorized all of the mistakes that women told her about, which fell into six or seven distinct categories including saving, spending, investing, and career issues. Then she shaped each of the categories in chapters. Frankel likes surveying because it enables her to conduct wider research. "It's important not to get stuck in your original paradigm," she declares, "because if you do, you can miss things that are on the periphery. Too many writers get so stuck in their own ways, they take such ownership of their words, that they don't think about whether the recommendations they make actually work or not."

Alison James set up surveys on her website. Although the information in her first book came primarily from her thoughts, her subsequent books were based more on information she obtained through surveys and interviews. In those titles, James included information from nearly twenty online studies, conducted about 150 interviews, and spoke with bright friends in depth. Her survey questions were not as sharply focused as Frankel's or structured like formal, academic studies, but were designed mainly to supplement information that she had already obtained.

Guy Kawasaki, author of *The Art of the Start* (Portfolio, 2004), has an email list that he uses to collect information. He will survey those on his list when he needs examples and feedback on what they would like to see in the book, and questions they would like answered. Casey Hawley also conducts surveys to get a consensus from people who are actively involved in the matters covered in her books.

Hawley conducts standard research, including Internet research, and tries to keep up with the best business books so that she knows what others are thinking. "Boy, the world changes, like, every six months, so I really try to see especially what people in other fields and people who are very different from me think."

Case Histories

Al and Laura Ries make it a point to collect case histories. The Rieses get histories from actual cases they handle in their consulting practice, from their extensive reading of business publications, and through their industry contacts. At their office, the Rieses keep fifty-four file drawers filled with case histories.

For the Rieses and many other authors, case histories are both sources of inspiration and raw material for their books. They make extensive use of case histories in their books because they provide graphic examples of points they want to make clear.

Case histories are wonderful teaching and learning devices because they are essentially stories that people identify with and remember. They make a strong impact on readers because they involve people, companies, and problems with which readers can relate.

My Least Favorite Part

The initial confusion that Leonard Koren goes through in book-writing projects is his least favorite part. Since Koren doesn't know where his books are going, he dislikes running into so many dead ends. He's also not enamored with the details involved in readying the book for the printer, such as copyediting and all of the double-checking and preparation involved.

Documentation

Train yourself to document your research so you can easily find the sources for the information you use in your books. When you conduct research, write:

- Accurate summaries of all information you find
- Exact, word-for-word transcriptions of quotations
- The precise name of the source of the information
- Publishing information such as the date of publication and the page numbers the material is contained on:

For example, *The San Francisco Chronicle*, March 25, 2006, p. B17.

The level of documentation you need will vary with the type of book you write. For, example, you may need more substantiation for facts you include in a historical book than for a collection of business sayings. For interviews and surveys, keep a copy of the questions you ask, the date they were asked, and when they were answered. If you record interviews, don't make digital recordings, but use tapes that you can label and keep. If you have to receive written permissions, keep copies of them.

"Documenting can be hard when you're researching and fascinated by the information you're finding," Charles Cerami confesses. "It's difficult to stop and make precise notes because it interrupts your reading and breaks your concentration. It keeps you from focusing on the content, which is your real interest."

When you're uncovering interesting information, you often can't wait to write about it, so you may not note the source. Then, if interruptions or distractions arise, you may forget to document your sources.

Although documenting as you research isn't fun, having to go back after the fact can be worse. If you have to return to verify sources three or four months later, finding what you need can be difficult and time consuming. Worse yet, you may not be able to find the sources, which can be a nightmare when you've built parts of your book around undocumented material.

So, religiously document as you research. Be disciplined; note your sources as soon as possible because taking the time to make note of them can save you substantial time and worry.

Action Items

1. State why it can be helpful to copy research findings into a notebook by hand.
2. What are the advantages of conducting constant research?
3. How is the Internet most valuable as a research tool?
4. How can interviewing experts be stimulating to writers?
5. Why is it important to document as you research?

·············· **REMEMBER** ··················

Research is an essential part of most nonfiction books. Many authors are always conducting research because they read constantly and extensively. Their reading generates book ideas and much of the content that they include in their books. Authors who constantly research consider it to be a part of their life and their natural curiosity.

As a research tool, the Internet is especially helpful in producing leads. It's also great for identifying books on your subject. Interviewing can produce in-depth information from acknowledged experts, add color, and provide vivid quotes. Other helpful research methods include conducting interviews and surveys and collecting case histories. When you research, save time and avoid problems by training yourself to document your research on the spot.

Chapter 8

GETTING ORGANIZED

Writing a book I have found to be like building a house.
A man forms a plan, and collects materials.
—James Boswell

This chapter covers:

- Why you must organize
- Minimum requirements
- Create a system
- Electronic notebooks and chapters
- File cards

Why You Must Organize

"Writing must be approached systematically: organization is essential," Brad Schoenfeld advises. "If you're not organized, it makes it difficult to develop a cohesive flow, and readers have trouble following writing that doesn't move logically, in a well-organized manner. Read and speak with people about organization and structure. Go to bookstores and libraries and study the organization and format of books to learn approaches you can use."

"Publishers are now doing less developmental editing. They copyedit, but many expect your book to be logical and well organized. If it's not, they may be unwilling to assign an editor to fix it, and instead, many will just pass and decide it's not for them," Schoenfeld warns.

From the time they first see your query letter or book proposal, agents, editors, and publishers will be paying close attention to how well you and your writing are organized. So, early on, organize yourself and create systems from which you can write your book.

Theodore Kinni spends a great deal of time organizing material before he starts writing because "the more it's organized, the clearer the material and the book will become." Organization helps Kinni write faster, with greater ease and flow. "If you sit down and try to start right out writing chapter one," Kinni notes, "it's much harder because you don't have the research. The main points haven't all emerged, so you don't have an outline and it's hard to write. As a result, it's easy to become discouraged. Writing a book is a front-loaded process because if you have the material, then the writing is faster and easier. However, it takes a huge amount of time and effort to put it all together."

Minimum Requirements

Before you start organizing, make sure that you know the minimum requirements that nonfiction books must have. Although all books differ and have diverse goals and objectives, at the least, all nonfiction must:

- **Have take-away.** Readers must receive some benefit. In most nonfiction books such as business, relationship, and how-to books, readers are not reading for pleasure, but to learn. Readers also want to learn from memoirs, biographies, and autobiographies while they enjoy a good read; they want to get something from every book.

- **Be logical.** Most readers, especially those who are reading to receive some benefit, don't have the time and patience to solve puzzles. They want books that contain information that they can easily follow, and they don't want to go through all the work involved in figuring out what an author is trying to say. Therefore, a book must hang together, be cohesive, and make sense.

- **Be readable.** Many authors feel that they have to impress readers. Some use jargon, pretentious constructions, and language that is difficult for most readers to understand. While some readers may be impressed, most will be turned off and won't continue reading. Since the primary objective of a book is to communicate, make it readable!

- **Provide something new.** With the exception of works written by the masters, no one wants to read the same old thing again. Although nonfiction books don't have to be completely original, they must contain enough that's new or different to interest readers. All it may take is updating a book to make it current, changing its format, or presenting its content differently.

Create a System

Find your own organizational system; whatever seems efficient and works for you. Make it logical and intuitive so that you can easily remember and understand how it works. Don't blindly copy other writers' logic because it may confuse you or take you forever to master. Stick with one system and don't switch back and forth; switching can get confusing, and valuable information could be lost.

Open a specific file, folder, envelope, basket, bin, or pile for each of your important topics. Then toss everything relevant into or onto it. Or, in the alternative, enter your research findings in computer files. Come up with logical names for your computer files and write a master list that contains all your project file names.

Collecting and organizing information starts the writing of the book. "The real art in writing any piece of nonfiction is the organizational process," David Fryxell discloses. "Figure out how things fit together and what buckets the information naturally falls into. Then, as you're gathering material, you can start organizing, categorizing and putting information into buckets. When you sit down to actually write the book, instead of having mounds of undifferentiated stuff that you can't even remember why you included in the first place, you will have a real sense of the general topics you want to cover. You will have like things sorted with the like, and it will give you a jump on the actual writing process."

As you get them, organize your research findings so they don't pile up and overwhelm you. Shortly after John McPhee conducts research, he types his notes and then photocopies them. He then cuts the photocopies into strips that have only one point on each strip. Then he places the strips in a manila envelope for that subject. The beauty of McPhee's system is that it allows him to focus on one topic at a time. If he's writing about geese, he pulls out the envelope labeled "Geese," removes all the strips, and places them in order. He doesn't have to worry about other chapters, only about organizing the inserts for the geese chapter, which he then uses to write.

"It helps to tackle one thing at a time and then move on to the next chunk and then the chunk after that," Fryxell advises. "If you keep it in an amorphous blob all the time, you'll have to constantly be leafing though it to find what you need. It takes a lot of discipline and work, but the payoff is that it makes the actual writing much easier. Since you have the information, you're free to concentrate on finding the right words and flow."

Fryxell places his materials in organized piles and creates detailed written outlines on yellow legal pads. If a quote that he needs is in his notebook on page 22, he inserts the number 22 at the appropriate place in the outline so he can quickly find it when he's writing. According to Fryxell, many writers get blocked when they can't get their hands on the facts or information they need. They get frustrated, detoured, and discouraged; they lose the flow and are taken out of the moment. They enter into "some sort of paper chase. Once they're out of the flow, it's hard to get that feeling back," Fryxell laments.

Collins Hemingway organizes online with folders and subfolders. He has huge files of e-mails and calls himself a horizontal filer because he spreads everything out. As a result, he doesn't have deep, jam-packed files, but lots of less densely stuffed files.

Leonard Koren keeps a notebook for each of his book projects. When he takes notes, he enters them in his notebook. Then he transcribes the notes from his notebook to his computer and organizes them according to how he thinks the book will be written. Koren realizes that his organization will probably change because his books usually go through many metamorphoses.

Judy Ford makes notes on strips of paper and on her computer. She always carries note cards and will wake in the middle of the night and jot down thoughts. Fabulous things come to her in the middle of the night. In addition, she writes down other things such as her favorite words, ideas, funny comments, quotes, et cetera.

Although Jay Conrad Levinson's research may produce scores of topics and ideas, he always initially organizes his books into just ten chapters. However, Levinson's finished books may contain more or less than ten chapters. Levinson feels organizing the book into ten chapters is the easiest way for him. "There is nothing magical in my starting with ten chapters; it's strictly a number that I can easily handle and it has no special or mystical significance. It's a structure, a starting point. General Patton said, 'Almost all plans fail, but you have to start with a plan,'" Levinson states.

Richard Narramore at John Wiley & Sons believes shorter and more impactful chapters truly elevate books. "My preference is for more shorter chapters rather than fewer longer ones. Today, readers have shorter attention spans and are less likely to read your book cover to cover. With a well-executed table of contents and shorter chapters, readers can jump around for just the parts that are more relevant to them. Write chapters like magazine headlines."

"I'm not a very systematic person," Malcolm Gladwell admits. "It's all very haphazard." He keeps computer notes but doesn't have a formalized system for keeping track of his notes. Gladwell has them scattered on his computer and when he gets into writing the book, he pulls them into a single file. He tends to work in little pieces. "I'll report and research a little piece and then write it and then put the piece somewhere and then go and do another piece and put the pieces together at the end," Gladwell reveals. He keeps all those little pieces on his computer so he can find them when he needs them. Gladwell doesn't open up an overall file for the book or project until the end, when he's putting it all together. When he works, each chapter is usually an individual file.

When Katherine Ramsland organizes a book, she opens a separate computer file for each of the chapters she listed in the book proposal's table of contents. She also imports the chapter summaries from the proposal to serve as outlines for the chapters themselves. Then she expands on them. As she works on the book, Ramsland will often change the content and/or the order of the chapters because of new information she receives when she attends conferences and speaks with experts. If they tell her about new developments, she tries to work them in.

When Ramsland organizes her materials, she identifies additional research she needs. First, she researches online and checks the extensive supply of books she owns. Then she goes to the library and conducts interviews. Ramsland tries to set aside time to read books and material on the subject so that she can immerse herself in her topics, which she feels helps her write.

As she organizes, Ramsland also decides what type of book she wants to write and whose cooperation she will need. Usually, she holds off writing content as long as possible, until she has a sense of wholeness about her subjects. Some take longer to become clear because she has to acquire a deeper sense about them. The depth of her immersion in the project helps her determine how she will approach the project, research it, and write it.

Ramsland puts the books and articles that she plans to refer to in the book in piles. As she reads information of interest, she will put it into an empty box that becomes her storage box for information on that book. Ramsland believes that this step is critical because after the book is submitted, an editor may want her to document or substantiate information or sources, so it's important to know where she can quickly find it. So she ends up with a storage box for each book she writes.

After Ramsland puts all of her research materials in piles, she organizes them in accordance with how she feels the chapters will unfold. She starts at the top of the pile and then goes through it. As she looks at an item, she decides how she should include and/or frame what she writes. Frequently, she will refer back to her own writing and similar information that she has written on the subject.

Before Al and Laura Ries begin writing a book, they discuss it extensively. They explore what specific chapters they should include and how each chapter should be approached. The most important step for them is agreeing on the chapter titles, which they feel frame and set the tone for the book, so they work on them together. The Rieses concentrate on what the chapters will be, what they will contain, and how they will be organized and flow. When all the chapters are organized, the Rieses then focus on each chapter individually. At that point, they know where to file their research findings and what information they must gather for the various chapters.

For content, the Rieses use the summary of chapters from their book proposal as a starting point. However, as they write, they always run into new information, so they constantly change chapter titles or even their order or content. They may add an additional chapter or throw one out completely. On occasion, they've changed the entire book.

For complicated chapters, Al will put the material in separate folders and then alphabetize the folders. He could end up with twenty-five to thirty folders that he can use. The Rieses continually organize intensively. They have fifty-four file drawers filled with case histories, and they get every business magazine you can imagine and five daily newspapers. Then they save those they want in folders. They are often sources of their inspiration and can be raw materials that they can go back and use. They supplement them with material from the Internet, such as statistics on current market shares and other figures.

Robyn Says

If you're highly organized, it will save you endless time searching for content. It will also help you plan for your book and subsequent books. When Rick and I began working on this Author 101 series, we brainstormed about the topics that we thought might fit in the series. First, we defined the overall project and made sure we looked at the big picture.

Ask yourself if your book could become a series. If so, what would you write next? What should you include in your first book that could save you time and work for future books? Think ahead.

My Favorite Part

Collins Hemingway's favorite part of the writing process is "being done. It's not easy for me. I don't know if it's because I'm getting to be a better writer as I get older and my standards are increasing as my abilities increase or it's just always hard. Writing has always been hard," Hemingway reveals.

Electric Notebooks and Chapters

Joseph Cardillo conducts research that is mainly internal. When Cardillo, who teaches creative writing and martial arts, settles on a book idea, he enters into his computer everything that could go into the book and sets it down as chapter headings. Initially, he doesn't place his entries in any particular order; he just lists them as they come to him. His primary concern is to inventory his ideas.

Cardillo then reviews his list to determine if he has enough substance for a book or whether his focus should expand or change. From his list, he can gauge how big the book will be and spot gaps that he should fill. Then he organizes the items on his list by placing them in categories. During this organizational stage, most of the items on the list find homes, but a few stragglers always exist. Cardillo then creates two additional types of files: (1) an "electronic notebook" and (2) chapter notebooks.

In his electronic notebook, Cardillo enters general information—anything from his experiences, observations, or thoughts. He scrolls through his electronic notebook every day and may add entries. He isn't discriminating, but tosses in whatever may have relevance: stories, facts, figures, information, ideas, and quotations.

To organize his electronic notebook, Cardillo numbers each entry according to when it came to him, not according to any logic or relationship to other materials. He also uses color. For example, if he believes an entry is especially important or knows that he will use it but isn't sure where, he will highlight it in red. He also puts critical items in twenty-four-point type so he can't miss or overlook them. Cardillo believes that graphic devices place ideas in his subconscious that eventually come out in his writing.

In addition to his electronic notebook file, Cardillo opens a folder for each chapter, in which he writes ideas and information that could work in that particular chapter. His objective is to place enough information in each chapter notebook that he can write the chapter from it. Cardillo has found this system invaluable at times, when he was too tired to write or was uninspired, because it lets him develop and refine existing material or add entries that he could subsequently write.

Cardillo's notebooks also make it easy for him to move material. If he comes across an item that doesn't belong in one chapter but that could work in a future chapter, he can simply cut it out and hold it in his electronic notebook or put it into the chapter notebook where it is a better fit. When the time comes to write a chapter, Cardillo reviews the information in that chapter notebook, organizes it, and then writes. As he does, he polishes his language and may add additional thoughts and information.

My Least Favorite Part

Working on the cover design is Laura Ries's least favorite part of a book-writing project. The problem is that she and her father, Al, have great ideas for covers, but the publishers don't listen. Frequently, the publishers show Al and Laura cover designs that don't really work because the designers who they farm the work out to don't understand what the books are about.

The more information Cardillo includes in his chapter notebooks, the easier it is for him to write the chapter because he has completed much of the work. "When you write a straight rough draft and then rewrite it over and over again," Cardillo observes, "you often tag onto the very first idea that comes to mind, which may not be your best idea. Then you start to develop that idea, which often goes nowhere, and it can discourage you. You may write it beautifully, but it isn't the best idea or it doesn't work as a lead for the chapter or the book."

"Working from electronic and chapter notebooks makes it easier to change direction because you haven't committed to so much actual writing," Cardillo adds. "You are also giving your subconscious more time and room to get involved in formulating how and what you write."

File Cards

Jean-Noel Bassior has a three-pronged organizational system. First, she prints out or copies information she has obtained from the Internet and notes she has taken at libraries, and writes up what she learned from interviews. Then she gathers up all of her research materials and numbers them. Bassior highlights the important information in her materials and writes a letter-number code in the margin next to them. Her code indicates the page of her research materials where the information is and the degree of its importance. For example, "55A" means that the information is on page 55 of her research and is top priority.

Second, Bassior makes an index card for each item of information. On the card, she describes the information and enters the code. This lets her glance at each card and immediately know where to find the source of the information.

Third, she puts on meditative music, sits down with a yellow pad, and tries to "see the larger picture that the book will tell." Since Bassior has transcribed her research findings onto index cards, she trusts that she knows the information she has collected, so she lets her subconscious mind put it in place. To do so, she thinks about each chapter and asks herself, "What is the plan for this chapter?"

Before long, Bassior is able to determine what information each chapter should contain, how it should be organized, and how it should flow. As it comes to her, she writes it on her yellow pad. Bassior concentrates on capturing the order of the chapter, not on language, and believes that her process lets the most creative part of her mind process information and place it in order.

As each chapter takes form, Bassior continues to develop and refine her thoughts. At some point, her opening usually becomes clear, which excites her because it crystallizes the chapter. Bassior knows her organization could change, but it doesn't bother her because she now has a format from which she can proceed. Bassior then shuffles her index cards, separates the cards by chapter, and places them in the order that she will follow in writing the book.

World-renowned Russian Novelist Vladimir Nabokov, the author of timeless novels like *Lolita, Pale Fire* and *Ada,* did his writing standing up, and all on index cards. This allowed him to write scenes non-sequentially, as he could re-arrange the cards as he wished. His novel *Ada* took up more than 2,000 cards.

Dr. Brenda Shoshanna also uses index cards. When she comes across information on various subjects, she enters it on index cards, which she sorts into different folders. She doesn't include her noodles, which she keeps in separate notebooks for each book. "It's very hard when you're writing a nonfiction book to hold everything in your head. So you want to write it down. People get overwhelmed. The more you write, the more thoughts and ideas it's going to generate—particularly during the noodling stage."

Rick Says

Collect and maintain information that can enhance your writing, such as quotations, sayings, facts, statistics, and interesting stories. These items are part of a writer's inventory because they add color, power, and credibility to words and content. Create a system that will make them easy to access when you need them. Keep records of all your sources so you won't have to waste time searching for them later.

As you come across interesting items, save them. Enter them in a computer file or folder or toss hard copies in a pile, a box, or a basket. Make it a regular practice to capture interesting items that you can subsequently credit or get permission to cite and potentially use.

Action Items

1. Name four ways in which you can keep your research information.
2. Draw a diagram illustrating how you want to organize the information for your book.
3. Explain why it's important to decide what your book's chapters will be.
4. Explain what an electronic notebook is.
5. State how an index card organizational system works.

·············· REMEMBER ··············

Have a system. Writing must be approached systematically because when it's not organized, readers have difficulty following it. Find a system that feels intuitive to you. Keep your research findings in files, folders, envelopes, baskets, bins, piles, or computer files. Give your computer files names you can easily remember and find.

Copy everything, even if you don't use it. Make copies of your research and cut them into strips that you can organize according to subject. Copy all of your information into notebooks, onto index cards, or into computer files, whatever will work for you. If you have a great many research materials, develop a code that will help you to easily access all of the information you collect.

Chapter 9

....

WRITING

....

I believe more in the scissors than I do in the pencil.
—Truman Capote

This chapter covers:

- Rituals
- Times and places
- Targets
- Main concerns
- Getting into the flow
- Writer's block
- Editing

For the purposes of this chapter, let's break down writing into two phases: composing and editing. The first phase, composing, is the initial creative stage when writers first express their ideas and information by writing them on a computer or on paper. The editing phase comes afterward. It's a second or review stage when the author, or an editor, examines his or her composition and makes changes in order to make it better. In this chapter, we will refer to the composing phase as writing and to the editing phase as editing.

Trying to describe the writing process is a major challenge. The subject is so enormous that we honestly don't know where to begin or where to stop. In addition, the process is individual, idiosyncratic; every writer approaches it somewhat differently and many vary from book to book, even within their books, so it's hard to determine what advice to give.

However, we strongly believe that no book on how to write nonfiction can be complete without examining the writing process because it's the moment of truth in literary art; it's when writers must perform, when they must put their words on the page. For most writers, everything else involved in a book project is preparation, an audition, a rehearsal, getting ready for the time when they actually sit down and write. To most, writing is when the magic occurs.

Award-Winning Author Walter Mosley says, "If you want to be a writer, you have to write every day. The consistency, the monotony, the certainty, all vagaries and passions are covered by this daily reoccurrence. You don't go to a well once, but daily. You don't skip a child's breakfast or forget to wake up in the morning."

"Every myth about writing, everything that you've been told has worked for someone else, can be a stumbling block if you don't see it for what it is—an individual approach, something that works for you and reflects who you are, how you like or need to work," Gregory Godek explains. "As a writer, you have many options. Look at twenty writers and you'll probably find that they're doing it twenty different ways. Study what other writers have done, how they did it, and how well it worked. But understand that their methods won't guarantee success for you. Experiment, try each of their techniques for yourself, but if they don't work, don't give up; try other approaches. Keep searching until you find a method that works for you. When you find your way, realize that your way is just as valid as that of anyone else."

So instead of trying to describe the writing process and tell you exactly what to do, we decided to outline how authors we interviewed proceed and to add a few words of our own.

Rituals

Some authors must religiously go through rituals before they begin to write. They may compulsively read the morning paper, play three computer games, or eat two and a half slices of cheese. Others may answer all their email, pay their bills, exercise, meditate, or put on certain music. Some need absolute quiet, a totally neat desk, and the perfect lighting before they begin.

Truman Capote claimed to be a "completely horizontal author." He said he would spend his time writing while lying down in bed or on his couch. He wrote his first and second drafts by hand. He would then switch to a typewriter, but would balance it on his knees while lying in bed.

Before Mary Roach starts to write, she puts in earplugs even though it's not noisy where she works. However, inserting the earplugs tells her that she is seriously into her writing.

Before Jeff Greenwald writes in the morning, he meditates. He also lights incense and plays music. He tends to meditate, read and answer his email, have breakfast, and then sit down to write. If Greenwald doesn't start by 9:00 or 10:00 A.M., he usually won't write much that day.

"People who put too much ritual into their writing by sharpening nine pencils before they write or whatever, are just procrastinating," David Fryxell believes. "At that level, especially for nonfiction, writing becomes a job."

According to an old saying, writers love to do anything except write. So, many procrastinate. Jay Conrad Levinson "procrastinates like crazy." He sleeps late and takes his time having juice, coffee, and reading the newspaper before he begins to write. He feels that his delaying clears his mind for him to write. When Levinson finally begins to write, he knows that he has everything behind him and he doesn't let anything stop him; he writes straight through. His family knows not to disturb him. If he takes telephone calls, he makes them very brief.

Often, when writers decide to write, they're just not ready. They may have other matters on their minds, be unclear how to plan their work, or have not fully organized the materials in their heads. When they procrastinate, they may be buying time to mentally better organize the information on which they plan to write.

So don't beat yourself up when you can't seem to write. Understand that you just may not be ready. Try to determine why you're not, and then try to fix the problem.

Times and Places

Writers can be rigid regarding when and where they write. Some will write only in the mornings, and many begin before dawn. Others prefer the afternoons or evenings or even work well into the night. Some are extremely flexible and write whenever they can steal time from the demands of their jobs, families, and other obligations. Find the time or times that are best for you.

Agent John Willig says, "One bit of advice I give my clients is not just to schedule a certain number of hours each day as writing time but to know what your best hours are and to block them from all distractions as your writing (and sacred) time. Some of us are morning people, others night owls. Whatever is your most energized and creative time of the day (if even for just a couple of hours) should be the time you devote to your manuscript and meeting important deadlines with your editor and publisher."

Judy Ford, who has a full-time counseling practice, writes every morning for at least three hours. Frequently, she has to force herself to sit down and write. When Leonard Koren is writing a book, he starts at 9:00 A.M. and works until 5:00 P.M., and he usually takes a break. Al and Laura Ries like to write in the morning, but they plan what they are going to write the night before.

Mary Roach typically writes in the afternoon. In the morning, she attends to email and calls. David Fryxell and T. Harv Eker don't have set times; they write whenever they can find the time in their busy schedules.

Award-Winning Collaborator Justin Spizman (www.justinspizman.com) updated this book in the evenings after he put his daughter to sleep. Because he has clients all over the world, he finds himself working at the oddest of hours. "I have had Skype calls with an Author in China at 2:00AM and then conference calls with a client in London that same afternoon. But I always make sure I wake up before my children do so I can write for those few quiet hours as the sun is rising. I find that time to be the most calm and collected for me and my mind."

Katherine Ramsland doesn't write at a set time. She will usually check her email before she starts writing. On days when she isn't teaching, she starts writing in the morning and writes until about 1:00 P.M. Then she exercises or runs errands. Usually, Ramsland starts writing again by late afternoon and will write deep into the night. She generally puts in at least eight hours a day writing.

Malcolm Gladwell likes to write in the mornings because he feels that's when he's most productive. However, the times when he writes can vary depending on what stage he's at, how he feels, and what other obligations he has. "I'm not an incredibly structured person; I kind of go with it. Sometimes when I feel good, I write a lot; when I'm feeling not as good, I don't write as much."

Gladwell takes frequent breaks. He will write for fifteen to twenty minutes and then take a little break. He frequently writes in cafes, which can be distracting. But sooner or later, he pushes projects forward and gets them done.

Robyn Says

I really enjoy writing in the morning, and I often will wake up extremely early just to write. It's so quiet and there are no distractions. If I can't sleep at night, I've found that writing in the wee small hours is an improvement over counting sheep. The key for me is to have a few projects in the works so I always have a place where I can apply my energies regardless of the time.

Some authors can write only while seated at their own desk and in their favorite chair. In order for them to write, all of their papers and reference materials must be placed exactly in the same spots. Others seem to do best in near chaos. A few writers told us that when they write, they can't handle any distractions, but most had learned to work through the normal interruptions and distractions of life. Some even felt that they turned out their best work in cafes, airplanes, the subway, or the bus.

Once many writers begin, they take infrequent breaks. Some work straight through the day. Others write for only short intervals; they jump around, pace, talk on the phone, instant message, and take a million breaks. They believe that frequent breaks help their minds organize and refresh.

When Leonard Koren writes, he keeps at it for however long it takes. Gregory Godek is an all-or-nothing person who likes to throw himself into things and do nothing else. However, Godek can't recommend his process to others. "Writing is so individual that the way you write should be based on you and your personality," Godek instructs. "Not based on a system or how everyone else works."

"It's hard to find what's right for you," Godek continues, "but if you really want to be a writer, you have to try, and keep trying until you find what's right for you. It involves a lot of hit and miss and trial and error."

Targets

Many authors try to turn out a certain number of words or pages each day. Others write strictly by the clock, for a stated number of hours. When they have been writing for a certain time, say five hours, they abruptly stop—regardless of where they are. Then, the following session, they pick right up where they left off.

In his book *On Writing*, Stephen King says that he writes 10 pages a day without fail, even on holidays. By contrast, Ernest Hemingway wrote 500 words a day. Both are highly accomplished authors who approached writing from entirely different points of view. The point is that there is no exact science. We all learn and execute information differently.

The prolific Jay Conrad Levinson tries to write between ten and twenty pages a day, depending on the book and the nature of the topic. Levinson can turn out all of that content because (1) he has done so much of his research up front that he can write rapidly, and (2) as a former advertising copyrighter, he was trained to write fast and to edit while he writes.

Katherine Ramsland doesn't set hourly goals for her writing because she knows that she will be writing frequently. Generally, she writes until she finishes the particular section or chapter on which she's working. Ramsland believes that her writing flows more quickly when she is learning as opposed to writing about matters she knows.

Mary Roach doesn't set goals for her output because she finds that "it makes you eternally neurotic and disappointed because you frequently don't meet the goals, especially when you need to do something else like go to the library to track something down." Roach finds trying to stick to a certain word count each day or week "kind of overbearing and depressing."

If Roach can write eight hundred words or more in a day, she feels good, and writing one thousand words a day can be a big motivating factor. "The less you write, the worse you feel," Roach points out. "It's a sort of internal monitor." She tends to write in "fits and starts" and doesn't write every day. For a while, she will write heavily and then she won't write at all for a few weeks.

When Roach writes, she tries to complete a chunk of research or a particular point. How much she writes is usually determined by the subject matter rather than by the size or the amount of her output. It can be a scene or a piece of information. Roach doesn't write chapters in a linear fashion, such as Chapter 1, then Chapter 2, followed by Chapter 3. Sometimes she will write blocks of interrelated chapters together when they have a strong connection.

For his first book, Malcolm Gladwell set concrete goals for how much writing he wanted to produce each day, but "I've gotten away from that. I'm less structured now than I was. I don't have any kind of strict deadlines; I just hum along and see how far I get. I'm pretty disciplined, so I don't tend to get behind. I try to do a little bit each day. As long as you can do that, you're fine."

When Jeff Greenwald is writing a book, he tries to devote three to five hours a day to his writing. He attempts to complete a modular portion each day. He may revise a chapter or two or write to a specific point. He will try to write a scene or scenes, write dialogue, and then he may call it a day.

Greenwald sets goals for his writing when he's writing a book. He assesses the size of each chapter and what it will contain and then he divides up how much he should accomplish each day. He puts together a rough flow chart on how he wants the writing to go.

Author 101 Advice

Some writers, including Jeff Greenwald and Katherine Ramsland, like to leave some of their work unfinished so they stop writing before they complete a section or a point. Then when they come back to their writing the next session, as Greenwald puts it, he "doesn't have to jump over that hurdle of writing again. I can just sit down and begin with something I know and from there, my momentum is already under way, and I can continue more easily."

Ramsland says, "It creates a pull that makes me want to get back into my writing." Most writers have difficulty with this technique because they're usually eager to finish their point or section. However, for others like Ramsland and Greenwald, it makes them look forward to writing again and completing the unfinished work.

David Fryxell doesn't set goals on how much or how long he will write. However, he's deadline driven. He will work backward and figure out that to make his deadline, he has so many days, which means that he has to write so much each day in order to make it. When he was writing his last book, he was also working a full-time job, but he tried to write one thousand words each night.

When Greg Godek starts writing a book, he tends to work on it for eight to ten hours a day for several months until it's done. But he would never advise others to write the same way.

Main Concerns

When Jay Conrad Levinson starts to write, his first concern is to get all of his ideas down. So he works from the chapter summaries that he wrote for the book proposal. He writes about and expands on all of the points and then, when he has covered them all, he goes back and edits what he's written. Usually, that one pass is the last editing he does.

In his writing, Levinson wants to clearly and simply present material about marketing that traditionally has been considered complicated. He wants to give readers a series of "aha" moments and make them realize that they can actually do what he writes about without professional help. Levinson tries to show readers that "it's not as complicated as they thought and that they can apply it to their businesses and increase their income, revenues and profits." His books are designed to increase his readers' business profits.

Katherine Ramsland searches for each book's "beating heart—when you feel its life and suspense." When she finds the "beating heart," Ramsland feels her writing is powerful, stirring, and energized; she knows that she has tapped into the life force of the book and it infuses excitement into her words.

As Alison James writes, she asks, "Who's going to buy this? What type of woman and why? Would I purchase this book and in what situations?" As T. Harv Eker writes, he continually asks what, where, how, and why. Then he answers each with an example or story. For each principle he gives and point he raises, Eker asks what is it, what is the point, why is it important, how do you do it?

Al and Laura Ries write the first sentence and then ask themselves, "What would the reader like to know next?" If the first sentence is a question, the reader will immediately want to know the answer. Many writers never answer the questions they ask; they use them only as rhetorical devices. The Rieses believe that with each sentence, writers must ask themselves what the reader would like to know next. Frequently, it will be examples of the claims or statements you just made.

In his books, Louis Patler strives to make each chapter modular so it is an end in itself that readers can read and understand. He wants readers to be able to open the book at any page and fully understand everything there. Patler believes that most nonfiction readers are busy, and they don't read nonfiction like they read novels. "They're usually looking for a little help, a little boost, a trick, or piece of information that they can put to use," Patler points out. To continually remind himself, he has a sign on his wall that reads, "It's better to be useful than correct."

Since Mary Roach isn't sure what her books are going to encompass, she writes the conclusions last and the introductions near the end. Recently she has been writing the introduction when she's halfway finished because she needs to know and express what it is she's writing, the direction she's taking, and what she hopes to achieve.

My Favorite Part

"My favorite part of the writing process is when my writing flows," Judy Ford announces. "I love those moments when a gorgeous sentence that you think you could never write comes out of nowhere and is so perfectly clear that it makes you say 'ah, oh wow.' It's like you're on automatic pilot, like a meditation, and to me, it's heaven."

Getting into the Flow

"Write what you know," says Geraldine Brooks, Pulitzer Prize winning Author. "Every guide for the aspiring author advises this. Because I live in a long-settled rural place, I know certain things. I know the feel of a newborn lamb's damp, tight-curled fleece and the sharp sound a well-bucket chain makes as it scrapes on stone. But more than these material things, I know the feelings that flourish in small communities. And I know other kinds of emotional truths that I believe apply across the centuries."

"I think that almost all writers would agree that the most inspiring thing is to start writing," Jeff Greenwald says. "Once you start writing, continuing is quite easy. Before you write those first words, that first sentence or that first paragraph, it's just really like being at the edge of a very cold lake that you're reluctant to jump in. But once you're in, the water is actually quite nice and after a few minutes of swimming, you're very comfortable."

Author Sylvia Boorstein wrote *Solid Ground: Buddhist Wisdom for Difficult Times* (Parallax Press, 2011) with a very specific set of guidelines. "When I settle into writing, I do not open email until 5PM on any weekday or other day when I expect to be writing; do not read other people's work on the same subject; I am very selective about having other people read it as I go along other than my editor; when I do not like how what I'm writing is sounding, I quit. I leave the computer. I do something else, like cook soup. I 'hear' what I am about to type before I type it and if it is not sounding like me naturally talking, I know I am not clear or balanced enough to go on; I do not write from the beginning to the end. I write in the order that particular parts take form in my mind and I enjoy mulling them over; I take the due date for the first draft seriously. Like everything depends on that day. It makes the project energetically alive for me, like a James Bond five-minutes-and-fifty-two-seconds until the whole world blows up movie and even if the draft is finished a week early I push the SEND button just after 12AM on the day it is due."

Each and every writer has his own process. There is no right or wrong answer. There is just a genuine drive to deliver the goods—a completed manuscript. Before you begin writing, consider how you work best. What are the conditions? The environment? The timing? Take those into account and sculpt writing guidelines so you can ensure you are actively working to optimize the process to your strengths.

David Fryxell goes chunk by chunk and writes to build momentum. "The writing process takes the discipline of putting your butt in the chair," Fryxell declares. When he writes, he has done so much homework that the process is very fast. "It comes smoothly and I don't have to go back and do a lot of revision." He tries for an A-minus first draft. He will do three or four hours at a sitting, either in the morning or afternoon. As he writes his first draft, he's editing to some extent. As he writes, he focuses on the rhythm of his sentences. He searches for the best way to express his material, and asks if he should start with a quote, where he should put the attribution, how much he should paraphrase, and what descriptions he should include?

Best-Selling Author Kent Haruf said, "After finishing the first draft, I work for as long as it takes (for two or three weeks, most often) to rework that first draft on a computer. Usually that involves expansion: filling in and adding to, but trying not to lose the spontaneous, direct sound. I use that first draft as a touchstone to make sure everything else in that section has the same sound, the same tone and impression of spontaneity."

As Brad Schoenfeld writes, portions of the book flow easily. He goes with this flow and tries to get as much down as he can. After a while, he usually has three different parts: (1) bits and pieces of the book that are fully written, (2) blocks where nothing is completed, and (3) notes that tell him what he needs to complete. As he starts filling in the pieces, other ideas come. "It's kind of like a puzzle," Schoenfeld reveals. "As you continue getting parts of it, the bigger picture begins to appear."

"You have a stack of material for each chapter," Al Ries observes. "And as you write, you find that some of the stuff you can use and others you can't. Once you've selected your material, then you have to find a hook—it's not just true of conceptual ideas, it's also true of sentences—you need a hook. Every sentence should hook to the previous sentence, and every question that's raised should be answered."

Judy Ford writes titles in a journal. Then she starts writing the first sentences and whatever comes to her. Pretty soon, a sentence will inspire her to write a paragraph. She works on several book ideas simultaneously until one begins to take the lead. She knows which book to write when the words, sentences, and ideas come together easily. And when she decides to write the book, she gathers up her journal entries, strips of paper, and computer writing and shapes them into the book.

"When I get a sentence that flows and expresses the message I wish to convey," Robyn notes, "it facilitates the next sentence. I like to write a few pages at a time and then reread and edit them until they feel right. I edit myself until I have nothing left to say. Then, the next day, when I return to the work, I'm always surprised when I reread it and find I have something new to add. Great writers avoid falling in love with their words until they flow perfectly. Underwhelm yourself; every word doesn't have to be perfect. Create substance, meaning, and flow."

Author 101 Advice

Dr. Brenda Shoshanna suggests that when writers complete the first draft of their books, they should celebrate. She suggests that they take time out to go for a wonderful meal, to the beach or the country, and give themselves some reward. Dr. Shoshanna feels it's important for writers to acknowledge that an important milestone, the first draft, has been completed, and to congratulate themselves. Then they can come back, with renewed vigor, and complete their books.

Writer's Block

In our interviews, we asked writers if they got writer's block. And we were amazed at how so few told us that they did. Most attributed it to the fact that they complete the bulk of their research up front, which makes it easier and more motivating to write.

Others considered it a matter of professionalism. Writing is their job, they reported. Several compared themselves to craftspeople because they have developed the discipline and the skills to complete the job at hand, which is writing. David Fryxell, who never gets writer's block, informs us, "Plumbers don't show up on the job claiming that they have plumber's block."

Malcolm Gladwell has a slightly different take. He has never has writer's block because he feels that his writing is straightforward work; he's not writing fiction or poetry. "I'm putting pieces together, like assembling a puzzle, and you don't have puzzle block when you're doing a puzzle," he notes.

Katherine Ramsland never suffers from writer's block because she loves writing and only takes on projects that she loves. Usually, she can't wait to get started on projects. Although Jeff Greenwald may have days when he doesn't feel like writing, he's never really had writer's block. He has never failed to produce a story or book that he was supposed to write. He may have times when he can't come up with inspiration or ideas, but never writer's block. Although it can be years between his books, he's not blocked during that time; he's just doing other things. Greenwald quoted Robert Benchley, who reportedly said, "I can only write when I'm inspired, and I make it my business to be inspired at 9 A.M. every morning."

Mary Roach never gets writer's block. However, she has days when it's hard for her to craft chapter openings because she wants to make the introductions so "kick ass." But days never go by when she can't write. When she has trouble writing an introduction or chapter opening, she usually skips it or just puts something there that she knows she will replace and then continues to write.

Writing sometimes is painful for Al and Laura Ries, but that's a part of the process. When their writing doesn't flow, they just keep writing. But they never really seem to have writer's block where they simply can't write.

On the rare occasions when Stedman Graham is blocked, it's more in the nature of a creativity block. At those times, Graham will leave the project alone and come back to it later. Over the years, he has learned that at times, he just can't be creative. So he just pulls back, focuses on something else, and then attacks it a while later with a refreshed mind. "You have to keep looking for that fuel that drives you," Graham suggests.

Virtually all authors have times when it's hard for them to write. However, the standard solution for them is to write: to sit down, tough it out, and work their way through. And in short order, they report, their fingers are usually flying and their inspiration returns.

If you have writer's block, interview others. Often, shifting your focus from your writing to obtaining information will break the logjam. Information you get through interviews and your interview subjects can be inspiring and help you write.

Editing

Editing is the process in which written compositions are reviewed, refined, and corrected to prepare them for publication. Writing involves constant editing and rewriting. You keep working with your writing until you shape it into what you want.

When writers work on book projects, they have come up with ideas and forms of expression, and many of them may not be valid or presented in the best way. So, during the project, writers must continually examine and evaluate the quality of their ideas and what they write. Frequently, they must reject, replace, and try to improve weak ideas, usage, and construction.

Remember, there is no shame in including a professional editor on your team. It can take a village to create a book. Just like working with a personal trainer, you will still have to do the heavy lifting. But, an editor may push you harder and require more responsibility and quality of work. Jonah Lehrer, author of *How We Decide* (Mariner Books, 2010), discusses his relationship with his editor. "My one piece of advice is to insist that your editor be brutal—there should be red pen on every page. At least in my experience, the book only gets decent during this phase, as all the darlings and digressions get killed. It's such an important process, and yet too many editors are too meek (or overworked) and too many writers resist their edits. A good editor is a great thing."

Rick Says

Most writers have trouble editing their own work. They know what they intended to say but may not be able to detect that they didn't actually say it or say it well. So, they tend to overlook their own mistakes. Publishing companies understand this and usually employ individuals to edit their authors' writing.

If you're not adept at spotting your own mistakes, work with an editor who can review your work before you send it in. A good editor can help your writing in numerous ways and make a dramatic difference in the quality of your writing.

Most writers self-edit as they write. They decide which words to use and the order in which they will use them. Writers continue to edit as they build sentences, paragraphs, sections, and chapters. "Experienced writers have usually learned the craft. So they have a stronger self-editing element in their writing," Katherine Ramsland observes. "They have learned to map out their words and sentences as they write, where it's a struggle for beginners or people who don't write regularly. Writers who write regularly—every day—have a stronger sense of structure, rhythm and grammar; so much of the editing process is built in by their experience. Experienced writers have the basics deeply ingrained, it's in them, it's a body memory, so they don't have to be so conscious of it, because they do it automatically."

When Dr. Brenda Shoshanna writes, she includes items that she hadn't originally planned to include. She moves straight through, from chapter to chapter, without heavily editing or revising and concentrates on getting ideas and information out. She doesn't go back and edit until she's completed an entire first draft, because she believes that writing and editing call upon different parts of her brain.

When Dr. Shoshanna completes her first draft, she takes a break from it and may not look at the book again for two or three weeks. Then she edits the entire book a chapter at a time. Usually, she makes two full editing passes that involve heavy editing and some revision. When she edits, she looks at the book with a structural eye and sees it as a whole. Between editing passes, she lets the book sit.

When Al and Laura Ries write, they edit intensively, even their first drafts, which they know will be heavily rewritten. They edit constantly as they write at every stage, for style, to make sure all material is in its proper place, and to avoid or deal with repetition. They don't want to tell the same story three times in slightly different ways.

The key to editing, the Rieses believe, is to make changes based on how readers will receive the material, not according to your thoughts. That's why it's so important to them to make sure that everything they write follows a logical sequence. Before they write, they always reread what they've written the previous day in order to remember what they wrote and to maintain the flow.

Malcolm Gladwell edits heavily as he composes. Then, when he finishes his first draft, he writes many subsequent drafts. "I'm very, very literative," Gladwell states. Usually, he picks up where he left off without editing what he previously wrote. He believes that if he edits his latest writing, he could end up just going back and redoing the previous day's work.

"I find that the thing that separates really good writers from less successful writers is that the really good ones do way more drafts," Gladwell declares. "They work harder on them. Some of the greatest writers I know will do fifteen drafts. When writers understand that it takes iteration after iteration, that's the way they get to be good. I think it's the thing that most young writers underestimate— how hard they must work on a piece."

Katherine Ramsland doesn't edit intensively as she writes. So she tries to write clear, fluid first drafts. She attempts to get the entire section or chapter down and to write everything she wants to say on that point. Then, after she has covered all of the important information, concepts, and blocks of material, she will reread and polish them.

"When I'm working on a book, the first thing I do in the morning when I sit down is to go over the introduction and first paragraph again. They're crucial to the book because they chart its direction." Reviewing these items keeps her on course; it reminds her of the direction she set for the book and helps her make sure that she has a compelling start for the book. It also puts her back in touch with the main thread of the book. Since most readers usually read the introduction or the opening paragraph first, they may be the most important pieces in getting readers hooked.

After Ramsland rereads the introduction and opening paragraph, she will occasionally review her writing from the prior day. But generally, she just starts writing where she left off.

When Jeff Greenwald composes, he edits intensively. He will go back and forth and edit a paragraph as much as a dozen times during the course of the first writing. By the time he finishes the piece, it's frequently ready to send out, and he has sent out pieces without making a final review of the versions he submitted. Generally, he prints out his compositions and asks friends who are not in the writing business to read and comment on them. Then he will revise them in accordance with their comments.

My Least Favorite Part

Mary Roach's least favorite part is realizing that how she structured a portion of her writing just doesn't work regardless of how much she tries to convince herself that it works. "It's the moment when you realize that you're going to have to go back, take it apart, and put it back together in a different way," Roach laments. "You thought you were done, but you're not."

Editing Prior Work

"When I sit down to work on a chapter, I usually begin by reading the last thing I wrote," Mary Roach explains. "I don't always read the entire chapter, because my chapters tend to be broken into two or three topical sections, but I usually read from the start of that section. It reacquaints me with where I stopped, what's in there, what I said, and where I have to go." Roach also finds herself editing the material she rereads.

As she writes, Roach edits intensively and constantly rewrites. Instead of writing a draft that she repeatedly works over, "I write a thousand microdrafts and am constantly changing, rearranging, rewriting. I'm very hard on myself," Roach reveals. "I revise and revise until I'm so sick of a chapter that I can't stand looking at it again, which is essentially when I stop. It makes me ill to read it again."

When David Fryxell starts writing, he reads over what he wrote the previous day. Usually, all he has to do is change a comma or a word or two here or there. Rereading the previous day's writing prepares him to write the next chunk.

Jeff Greenwald occasionally reads what he has written the day before, but he doesn't do it all the time. Usually, he just moves forward. "You can endlessly revise and rewrite. At a certain point, you just have to let go and move on to what you have to do next. There is really no limit to how much you can improve things, and you eventually learn that countless revisions and editing don't necessarily improve what you wrote, they may only change it."

For Leonard Koren, writing is rewriting; trying to refine and clarify what it is that he's trying to say. His initial objective is to get his thoughts on paper. His books require thoughtfulness at every moment, so he tries to articulate the ideas as clearly as he can and then he goes back and expresses them even more clearly and simply.

Just Getting It Down

When Koren writes, he tries to complete whole sections or chapters on the first pass, without editing. His objective is to capture as much of the "totality" first and then he will go back and edit it. According to Koren, editing intensively as he writes would be obsessive, which is a dead end for him. When he becomes obsessive, he knows that some insecurity is driving him and it never comes to a good end. So he tries to relax, approach it as a single entity, and then come back and work through it from beginning to end.

"I know that I'll make many passes over the same piece of paper, so I don't worry about the final expression. I try to collect as many elements of the constituent idea at that moment and I know from experience that there will be innumerable things that I've neglected or misrepresented. So I constantly have to go back over it. I'm never looking for the perfect word or the perfect literary feel for the work, I'm concerned on idea level. If there is a visual image that I have in my mind, I want to communicate the concept in my mind to the reader's mind. The words are not superfluous, but I don't consider myself a wordsmith because I find myself steering away from that. I don't want my words, my language to be too pretty."

Action Items

1. List the rituals that you go through before you write or how you procrastinate.
2. Identify when you do your best writing, at what time of day?
3. Keep a record of how much or how long you write each day, and if you could do more?
4. List your three top concerns for your writing.
5. If you get writer's block, identify the circumstances.

·············· **REMEMBER** ··················

Create your own process. Approaches and techniques that have worked for other writers can be a stumbling block for you. Writers have many options, so you must experiment and try various methods for yourself to see what works best. Many of the rituals and much of the procrastination that writers go through may be to allow their minds to clear so that they are ready to write.

As you experiment, find the times when you write best. Also, find a good place where you can concentrate on your work. Decide if you want to set goals as to how long you want to write or how many words or pages you hope to produce. If you complete your research before you begin to write and approach writing professionally, you may be able to avoid writer's block.

Chapter 10

....

MAKING IT SPECIAL

....

The faster I write the better my output. If I'm going slow I'm in trouble.
It means I'm pushing the words instead of being pulled by them.
—Raymond Chandler

This chapter covers:

- Covers
- Titles and subtitles
- Design
- Working with a designer
- Writing approaches

According to estimates, over 300,000 new books and editions were published in 2011, so the market for books is densely crowded and quickly growing. In fact, this number has doubled since 2004, when the first edition of *Author 101* was released. To interest publishers and readers, your book has to be distinctive and special, otherwise it will probably never be read.

To make your book special, use every weapon in your arsenal; pull out all the stops. After you've clearly and intelligently written about all of your essential points, impress agents and publishers with the full extent of your creativity and talent. Show them that you not only write brilliantly, but that you also have great, innovative ideas and that you will work tirelessly to make your book a gigantic success.

Read extensively. Go to libraries and bookstores and note the qualities in books that you like and try to incorporate them in yours. Take time to browse through sites like Amazon.com and review the market and those books that are regularly selling. Since books are now your business, study them from a new perspective. Examine book covers, titles, subtitles, designs, approaches, and writing styles to find the elements you like and that could work well for your book.

Although most publishers insist on the right to decide on book covers, titles, and designs, give them your ideas. If you're talented in any of those areas, offer your ideas and recommendations. Some may consider your suggestions and may even adopt those that could help your book.

If you plan to self-publish, the title and design of your book are of critical significance because they impact sales. The designs of many self-published books are amateurish at best, which makes them look unprofessional and turns off potential purchasers. Neither buyers for bookstores nor the public take them as seriously as well-designed, professional-looking books. Consider hiring a professional designer who has experience designing books.

Covers

The look of a book's cover is important because it's the first thing prospective readers see. Readers usually notice covers before they read titles or have any idea what the books are about. Covers give readers their first impression of books. If a book has a good look and feel, browsers will be more likely to pick it up and examine it more closely.

Study the covers of similar and competing books. Look through the stacks and find a bunch of books with covers you like, put them in a pile, and make notes on what attracted you to them. List the colors, typefaces, sizes, and graphical devices you like; also note what you dislike. Identify elements that you would like to incorporate into your book's cover.

Although she knows that publishers usually retain the sole right to determine a book's cover design, Robyn submits her ideas with her book proposals. Many publishers are open to input from authors, and while they don't always go with Robyn's suggestions, they frequently incorporate parts of them in the final covers.

"For one book, I actually mocked up the entire cover on my computer," Robyn discloses. "Then I cut and pasted it and voila. It was a rough idea, but I presented my case visually and they went for it. If you hate a cover design, contact your agent. Get his or her opinion and ask him or her to argue your case with the publisher. It will add credibility to your request."

Your book will be judged by its cover. Try to get a cover that:

- Pops off the shelves
- Can be seen easily when shown in the media, where it may be reduced to the size of a postage stamp

Submitting suggested cover designs helps publishers more fully understand your vision of your book. It may also awaken them to ideas and possibilities that they hadn't foreseen. If you're visually or graphically gifted, you are also giving publishers the benefit of your talent, which most publishers and their design departments will gladly accept.

Make your cover design suggestions early because many publishers contract their covers to outside design firms. When they have paid a firm to create your book's cover, they may be reluctant to replace it with a design or even elements of a design that you subsequently suggest. However, if you give them your suggestions before they incur any outside expense, they may be more receptive to your ideas.

Be constructive with your suggestions. Rather than saying, "I don't like the cover," politely offer suggestions regarding what the publisher could do to improve it. "Could we try larger type for the title, colors with a higher contrast, like more black and white, and my picture on the jacket flap?"

If your book is on, or features, art, illustration, or photography, consider insisting on design control. Most traditional publishers won't accommodate you, but some specialty houses might. They may agree to consult with you on designs but still insist on making the final decisions.

If the quality of the reproduction in your book is important to you, check the books produced by different publishers to identify those that consistently meet the standards you want. However, a house's track record may not guarantee the quality of reproduction for your book because publishers may work with different printers.

My Favorite Part

For Leonard Koren, the best part of the book-making process is the very beginning, when he really doesn't know where he's going. "The world is open to me. It's the same sense of adventure that must be felt by a mountain climber who is about to ascend to a place he has never been. It's an adventure, and the sense of impending discovery is wonderful," Koren discloses.

Titles and Subtitles

Book titles sell books. Like great ideas, they're the grabbers that attract immediate attention; they make people stop and take notice. Great titles convince publishers and readers to buy books. When they spot books with great titles, browsers often will pick them up and examine them to see what they contain, which increases the chances that they will buy them.

People remember great titles, even individuals who seldom read. People also like to tell others about terrific titles—it's like repeating a good joke. A good title generates publicity for the book, and readers tend to remember it. And when they go to a bookstore, they are more likely to buy books with titles they recall.

A great title may not explain what the book is about; it may only capture people's interest. For example, how many people could tell what *The Tipping Point* was about when they first heard the title or read it on the book's spine? Yet that phrase has now entered the language and is regularly used by people who have never read the book.

When a title doesn't communicate what the book is about, it needs a descriptive subtitle. The key to subtitles is that they must be totally clear. While the title is intended to be a hook that grabs readers' attention, the subtitle is intended to inform readers what the book is about.

When readers come across clever, interesting, and thought-provoking titles, it whets their appetite; it draws them in. They frequently presume that the book will be good since it was written by the same person who came up with the title. If the subtitle is descriptive, it can close the sale.

Robyn Says

Your book title will become your calling card; it will be attributed to you and identified with you. Treat it as your brand—consider it the centerpiece of the ad campaign for your book. Will it have sustaining power? Almost thirty years ago, I coauthored a book titled *Good Behavior* with Drs. Stephen and Marianne Garber, (St. Martin's Paperback, reprint edition, 1993), which has been in print for over three decades and its title still holds up. Create an instantly recognizable brand name that stands out and delivers a powerful message.

Titles are usually extensions of book ideas, but many writers come up with their title first, and the title inspires them to write the book. A great title embodies and crystallizes the idea of a book. Alison James feels that "The book title can make all the difference in the world. It has to be more than appropriate; it has to grab potential readers and cause them to react. There's a delicate balance: you have to have the right idea; it has to be a strong idea and feel right to you. It has to seem right in light of what's already out there and you have to have the right packaging." When James begins a book project, she needs to see the title up front to be sure that it is a book that she wants to write.

"A great title becomes a spark that can take all of your research, stuff that may be unconsciously floating around in your brain, and give it a direction, focus or context," says Gregory Godek, author of *1001 Ways to Be Romantic*

(Casablanca, 1995) and thirteen other books. If the title doesn't express the concept of the book, and many great titles don't, the idea should be explained in the subtitle. In such cases, the title introduces the book, but the subtitle explains what it's about.

Book titles are always swarming around Judy Ford's "head like bees around a honeycomb." She loves and thinks in terms of book titles. Ford gets the title first; it crystallizes ideas and approaches she has been thinking about, and then she develops the book around it. She keeps a list of titles and thinks about which one she wants to write next.

Find a great title and subtitle for your book, but understand that it may be only temporary. Most book publishers insist on the right to choose their book titles; they may change yours without your consent. However, agents recognize and love great titles, and a great title can get them to give more consideration to your book.

Design

Book design encompasses several aspects: cover design, which we've addressed; the book's format, and its interior design.

The format of a book can be an important selling point because it governs how the book's information is presented to readers. Since most nonfiction books are written in a logical narrative sequence, books that are structured as lists, rules, or by other classifications can also be highly effective.

In instructional books, the usual narrative chapter format can be dry, and busy readers may feel that they don't have the time to read them sequentially. So, they may be drawn to books that give them smaller blasts of information.

A book's interior design can be even more critical. Densely packed pages are intimidating; readers don't like to read them. And books should be inviting because readers have so many other options besides reading your book.

The interior design of many self-published books is poor. Everything is scrunched together; the pages are black, dense, and hard to read. The paragraphs are tightly packed, and readers feel that they don't have places to stop and breathe. Breaks that help readers, such as bullet points, boxed or shaded stories, sidebars, and frequent subheads, are often absent. If you plan to self-publish, consider hiring a professional designer.

Working with designers can be touchy. Good designers have vision and a unique style, but they may also have a big ego. Writers' and designers' sensibilities can clash. Authors seldom talk about their expectations, and designers frequently don't ask.

Working with a Designer

To work harmoniously with a book designer, Gregory Godek suggests that writers use what he calls "three rounds of three." Here's how it works.

Find a designer you like. Start with the cover design. Clarify your expectations by telling him or her that you want him or her to design three covers and for each of the three covers you want:

1. **A cover similar to what you think a major publisher would produce.** Find some covers that you really like that big publishers have created and show them to the designer.
2. **A cover that you think you want.** Tell the designer what you think should be included in the cover to incorporate your vision, style, and feelings about your book. Show the designer covers you like, as well as typefaces and other design features.
3. **The designer's best idea for a cover.** Tell the designer to go wild and do whatever he or she wants, to be creative but on target, and come up with what he or she thinks would be best. Give him or her the freedom to produce a cover that you would never have imagined.

Have the designer submit a cover for each of these categories, and discuss with the designer what you like and dislike about each. Then go through the process for two more rounds, in which the designer produces a cover for each of the three categories. By the third round, Godek feels certain that you will have a cover design that you will both like and that should work.

When you agree on the cover design, the interior layout should be easier. Again, show the designer samples of interior designs that you like and dislike. Then ask for him or her to give you three samples. From the three, you should be able to get what you like.

Writing Approaches

No matter what you write, Peter Bowerman, author of *The Well-Fed Writer* (Fanove Publishing, 2004), says, "It must have a unique selling proposition; something that differs from other comparable books. Know your unique selling proposition, how your book is unique, and make sure that your readers also know it." Specifically tell them how and when your book differs.

The following approaches can help you make your nonfiction writing unique. Think about each of these items and then determine how you could incorporate it into your writing. They include:

Be Clear

Whatever you write must be clear. If you have something worth writing, present it so it will be fully understood the first time readers read it. If readers can't follow what you write, what's the sense? You've wasted both your and their time.

Clarity is the first and most important rule of nonfiction writing. As a nonfiction writer, your main job is to clearly communicate to your readers; it comes before demonstrating how smart you are, how much you know, how clever you may be, or your style. Every part of your writing should be structured to make the meaning of your writing clear and easily understood.

Rick Says

Many writers want to impress readers with their knowledge, so they litter their writing with big words, long sentences, and complex language. They may also talk down to readers or confuse them with theories that blur what they write.

Carefully select every word you write and how you use it so that it clearly expresses what you want to convey. Try to communicate, not to impress. Note when you include terms that are commonly used in your industry and make sure that they will be readily understood by readers who are not in that industry or familiar with those terms.

In instructional, how-to books, provide enough detail to clearly and fully describe each process involved. Don't take shortcuts or just tell readers what to do, instead show them by explaining how they can accomplish every step. Foresee all options and decisions readers may face. Identify where they could go wrong and tell them how to avoid potential mistakes. Be explicit and understandable.

Break your writing down into smaller categories and subcategories, little chunks that focus on particular areas. Smaller portions are easier to digest, less intimidating and overwhelming. They're easier for you to write and for readers to understand.

My Least Favorite Part

Rewrites are Dr. Dan Baker's least favorite part. He feels it becomes tedious and like pulling teeth. "You have to watch your ego and put it aside," Baker notes. "You must realize that your editors are a part of your team, and their suggestions, as difficult as they may be to take, can make your book more understandable or direct it to a broader group of readers."

Your Voice

Write your book in a conversational tone by letting your own natural voice come through. We all have uniquely personal voices, so write as you speak and don't adopt anyone else's style, voice, or language, because it may not ring true. Most readers of nonfiction want to feel that they are in a conversation with the author; they don't want to be lectured to or to have the subject matter obscured by the way the writer writes.

When you write, your objective should be to have readers say, "Reading your book made me feel like you were sitting and talking to me," Peter Bowerman reports. "An engaged reader will continue reading your book, will understand it, praise it and spread the word. Don't lecture or be condescending. Be conversational."

Listen to your words and those of the people with whom you speak. Concentrate on the way they talk, the words they use, and how they utter them. Take notes and then work them into your writing to make it more conversational.

Before you begin to write, think about the voice you want. Don't delude yourself into thinking that you can be an invisible narrator, because your voice will seep through. Decide on the voice you want and then work to perfect it.

For example, determine if you want to be humorous, nonjudgmental, positive, optimistic, inspiring, authoritative, etc.

In your writing, use the words that you use when you speak, but be precise and distinctive. Identify objects instead of referring to them as "things" or "stuff." Paint a portrait by using visual images, references, and descriptions.

Develop a conversational tone by reading your writing aloud. Learn to objectively listen as you read and to determine if your writing genuinely sounds natural and conversational. Most writers write with their ears, by listening to how their writing reads.

"You can't be a writer; you have to be a person first and then write," Al and Laura Reis explain. "You have to live life, have the experience, and then write about it. To write business books, you have to be a businessperson first and then a writer second." The Rieses' writing is a spin-off of what they've learned and experienced in business. It contains the same information that they tell their clients, such as what works and what doesn't.

Reveal Yourself

Include stories and anecdotes; when possible, open with them. Many readers skim over the text and closely read the stories. Stories and anecdotes capture readers' attention when they leaf through books. They provide vivid examples and make content easier for readers to absorb, relate to, and retain.

Use yourself as an example and be willing to reveal yourself. Show your readers that you've worked through the struggles and experiences that you're writing about, that you've been there and understand. Expose yourself with all your blemishes.

Dr. Lois P. Frankel writes from her heart. If she just writes from her head, she feels, readers won't want to read her writing. Readers love stories; they want to hear your experiences and other people's experiences because they can identify with them. So she tries to appeal to readers' hearts rather than to their intellects.

"The best books reflect the writer's heart and essence, but they also provide benefit for the reader," Robyn points out. "While readers love writing that comes from the author's heart, it's usually wasted if it doesn't give readers' benefits. When writing combines both, heart and benefits, it's an unbeatable combination."

When it comes to revealing his heart and soul through his stories, Mitch Albom says, "When time came for me to write something after *Tuesdays with Morrie*, I moved slowly. I didn't want to do any sequels. No "Wednesdays with Morrie." No self-help series. I wanted to return to the world of stories, to delve deeper into life and death and the connections between the two - which lead me, inevitably, to the idea of heaven. Somewhere, swimming in my head, was the image my uncle had given me around that table, a handful of people waiting for you when you die. And I began to explore this simple concept: what if heaven was not some lush Garden of Eden, but a place where you had your life explained to you by people who were in it—five people—maybe you knew them, maybe you didn't, but in some way you were touched by them and changed forever, just as you inevitably touched people while on earth and changed them, too. And so, one predawn morning, coffee in hand, I sat down to write my next story, which now, several years later, is presented to you. It's a tale of a life on earth. It's a tale of life beyond it. It's a fable about love, a warning about war, and a nod of the cap to the real people of this world, the ones who never get their name in lights. This story is also a personal tribute to my uncle, whom I only wish could be here to read it."

Write nonfiction that is as interesting as fiction by using tools that are common to best-selling novels. It will help your nonfiction come to life.

- Write more in scenes.
- Use quotes as dialogues.
- Provide more description.
- Capture the graphic details and work them in.
- Give sensory details.
- Become a good observer. Then explain what something or someone looks like, how they sound, gesture, and move.

"Train yourself to be a good observer because it can lift your nonfiction into the realm of an art," David Fryxell suggests.

Author 101 Advice

Make the first sentence of your book outstanding because it's what visitors to Amazon.com see. Think of your first sentence as the equivalent of a sound bite or elevator speech. However, Mary Roach warns writers not to get hung up on leads because it can derail their writing. "Just write filler," Roach recommends, "like dentists who put in temporary fillings. Throw in any old lead and then come back to it. It's actually easier to write a lead after you know what you're introducing."

When Gregory Godek struggles for a word, he leaves a blank space or puts in a weaker word and flags it. Then, he comes back later and replaces the weak word with something better.

Provide Benefit

Readers want to learn, which isn't always easy. In fact, it can be difficult. Books can be intimidating, especially when their subjects are new to readers. "People don't just want to read theory, and publishers don't just want theory. It should have take away," Dr. Lois P. Frankel points out. "So provide value and benefit to your readers."

Many readers want to learn about themselves, not just a topic. The ultimate benefit can be when they learn about themselves in relationship to the subject. Including self-assessments, action items, and checklists can help readers measure what they've learned and help to motivate them. This draws readers more into books and makes the books come alive for them. They can also evaluate how it applies to their particular situation and how they are going about handling it.

Motivate and inspire your readers. However, don't constantly be a cheerleader or give readers pep talks because they will stop believing you and skim over what you write. Instead, help readers succeed by giving them clear directions that they can easily follow. Nothing is more motivational or inspiring than success.

Action Items

1. Explain why having a great book design is so important.
2. Describe the main function a book's subtitle should perform.

3. Explain how Gregory Godek's "three rounds of three" works.
4. State the first and foremost rule for nonfiction writing.
5. State the techniques from fiction writing that you could use in your book.

·················· **REMEMBER** ··················

Make your book special by suggesting great cover and interior designs and a fabulous title. Your publisher may insist on making these decisions, but also may be open to your suggestions, especially if they're strong. Include a subtitle that clearly conveys what your book is about.

The top priority for your writing should be to clearly communicate the material in your book. Write your book in a conversational tone by letting your own natural voice come through. Use stories and anecdotes as examples and incorporate techniques from fiction to give your nonfiction life. For example, write more in scenes, use quotes as dialogue, and provide more description.

Chapter 11

COLLABORATION: HOW IT WORKS

Some collaboration has to take place in the mind . . . before the art of creation can
be accomplished. Some marriage of opposites has to be consummated.
—Virginia Woolf

This chapter covers:
- Filling weaknesses
- Finding a collaborator
- Drawbacks
- Working together
- Anatomy of a collaboration

Filling Weaknesses

Writing can be lonely and isolated work. You can spend endless hours day after day, month after month sitting by yourself in front of the computer thinking nothing but your own thoughts and seeing only your own words. Working with someone else can be both enjoyable and productive.

Writing and publishing can also be demanding. You may have a fabulous book idea that everyone can't wait to read, but you lack the time to research and write it. Or you might not have the credentials to write a book on a particular subject even though you may have extensive knowledge about it. So you may have to collaborate and share the credit with a well-known authority or expert.

To succeed in today's market, you must start with a great, salable book idea; have excellent credentials; write well; and vigorously promote your book. And, as we have mentioned, publishers are becoming increasingly insistent on acquiring books written by authors who have national platforms.

Collaboration is often the ideal solution. Sometimes, it's the only way you can get your book written and/or published. You may want to write about the remarkable energy-saving system you developed, but you don't write well. The agents and publishing companies that were begging for a glimpse of your book take a quick look but then send it right back to you. Finally, you get the message: you could use some help.

You may be a perfect candidate to work with a collaborator, a writer who could help write your book. That person could be a coauthor, who could write the book with you, or a ghostwriter, who would write it with or for you. You could pay that individual a fee, divide the income the book earns, or work out a combination of both.

"An advantage of collaboration is playing up each other's strengths," according to Tory Johnson, who collaborated with Robyn on the *Women for Hire's: Get-Ahead Guide to Career Success* (Perigee Books, 2004). "Maybe one of you is a top-notch researcher, and the other is a solid writer. One might be great at conducting interviews, and the other prefers to stay behind the scenes putting it all together. Figure out your roles before deciding to move forward with any book."

Robyn Says

A great collaboration requires all partners to be concerned about each other's success, not just their own. Like a business with co-owners, the business, or the collaboration, must come first. Learn what your collaborator values and treat each other with respect. Make sure to define your respective roles and bring your efforts, creative ideas, and a sincere desire for a mutually beneficial relationship to the table.

Although editors, illustrators, designers, and other specialists can make great contributions to your book, this chapter addresses only collaboration between writers.

Finding a Collaborator

The first step in finding a collaborator is knowing precisely what you want. Since collaboration is a partnership, find a compatible collaborator, someone whose strengths will offset your weaknesses. If writing isn't your strength, you probably will want to collaborate with an accomplished writer. However, since writers write in many different styles and specialize in diverse areas, make sure that you find a writer who can write the type of book you want.

Johnson comments, "As the CEO of Women For Hire (*www.womenforhire.com*), which is the leading producer of high-caliber recruiting events throughout the country that connect professional women with leading employers, my area of expertise is writing practical, user-friendly advice and inspiration specifically for women on how to get jobs and advance their careers. In 2001, after researching experts in Atlanta who would be the ideal candidate to feature at my event, I invited Robyn Spizman to appear and sign her books. After seeing Women For Hire in action and the service we provided women who attend, Robyn approached me to coauthor a book. I was fully aware of her expertise and track record. No amount of career-related knowledge or expertise on my part would have resulted in books had it not been for her guidance, connections, and know-how in the publishing world. She instantly recognized my passion for helping people get jobs, as well as my platform for reaching women. Simultaneously I was in awe of her publishing and promotion strengths and we knew that we'd be ideal publishing partners. Spizman and I have always clicked. We value each other's opinions and communicate daily about everything related to our joint projects—from titles and editorial direction to sales and promotional opportunities. Having met many people in the book world, I know this isn't always the case. The partnership that Spizman and I share is unique and I cherish it."

Rick Says

If you're a writer who wants to launch or boost your writing career, collaborating can be a great way for you to get a book credit under your belt. Being a published author can establish your career, and collaborating can be the ideal way to get the experience of writing a book. It can also help you make valuable contacts and demonstrate to agents, editors, and publishers the quality of your work and that you have the ability and dedication to write a book.

The best way to find collaborators is through people in the industry such as agents, other writers, writing instructors, and publishing professionals. They usually know the talent in the field; who is good, their specialties, and what they've done. Also check with your network contacts and their network contacts, your friends, family, and associates. Ask former teachers or acquaintances who may work in writing and publishing as well as writers' organizations and groups. Specializing in non-fiction, self-help, and business development books during the course of his career, Justin Spizman works directly with authors who have worked hard to build their platforms.

Never forget that you will be entering into a business relationship with a collaborator that could extend for months or even years. If a book that you write with a collaborator is highly successful, your legal rights and the financial returns could outlive you.

Although partnering always involves risks, try to protect yourself by getting references and recommendations on all potential collaborators. Speak with those who worked with them and find out how successfully they worked together.

When you approach people for referrals to collaborators, specifically ask them:

- Rank how this individual was to collaborate with on a scale of 1 to 10, with 10 being the highest.
- Can you give me, or where can I obtain, samples of his or her work?
- What did he or she do best?
- What were his or her weaknesses?
- Was he or she punctual and dependable? If not, please explain.
- Rank the quality of his or her writing on a scale of 1 to 10, with 10 being the highest.
- Did he or she listen to your opinion and feelings?
- Was he or she open to your input and suggestions?
- Was he or she pleasant, reasonable, and accommodating?
- What could he or she have done better?
- Was he or she always accessible to you?
- How long did it usually take for him or her to respond?
- Did he or she give clear, responsive answers to your questions?
- Did he or she truly understand your goals and values?
- Did you have any financial disputes? If so, what were they?
- Is he or she honest and fair?
- Would you collaborate with him or her again?
- Who else would you suggest I contact?

When you get the names of potential collaborators, meet them in person if at all possible. If they are in different locales, speak with them by phone. Ask to see samples of their work and review them closely; ask for the names of the people they worked for and the right to contact them.

Trust your instincts when you speak with potential collaborators. Collaborations are much like business partnerships with the finished product of this partnership coming in the form of a manuscript. So, it's critical to quickly assess in the beginning the different writing styles and voices of the authors to blend them into one consistent and powerful voice. These concerns should be discussed and evaluated at the beginning of the process rather than during or at the end of it. Oftentimes, this can create misunderstandings and disruptions. Place great weight on whether you think they can do the job and if you like them, feel comfortable with them, trust them, and think that you could work compatibly with them.

Specifically ask:

- Do you specialize in a particular genre of books?
- May I see examples of your work?
- Can you write in _____ style?
- How will you capture my voice?
- May I have a list of your current and past clients?
- May I contact your clients?
- Will you sign a written collaboration agreement?
- What specific services will you provide?
- Do you agree that I will have final approval on all decisions?
- How long will it take to complete your services?
- What can I do if I don't receive the results promised?
- Can I fire you?
  - o If so, when?
  - o Will you still be entitled to fee payments?
  - o If so, for what and how much?
- What are your strengths and advantages over other _____?
- Who are your favorite writers?
- Are you familiar with the following books?

_____

_____

Base your decision on trust and communication: give great weight to the fact that you trust him or her and feel that you communicate well. Discuss your values with each other to determine whether you share common values and objectives for both the book and life. Understand that you're entering into a relationship in which you will be working closely and depending upon one another.

My Favorite Part

David Fryxell often thinks that his favorite part of the writing process is the organizing process because it's "where the real art is." However, in practice, he enjoys the actual writing most because the hard work has been completed and it's fun seeing the book come to life. "It's like putting flesh on the bones of the outline, which is exciting," Fryxell observes. "It's seeing that all my hard work is really working and coming to life on the page."

Drawbacks

Any partnership can have problems. In book collaborations, the two most common difficulties involve performance and ego. A partner may not carry his or her load, which can cause the burden to fall on the other and breed resentment. Regarding ego, one of the collaborators, frequently the one who conceived the idea, may feel that it's his or her book and want or take all of the credit. Another problem that often arises is when one of the parties does not take criticism well and is not open to suggestions and advice.

In collaborations, the status of the parties is often unequal; one of the parties usually takes the lead and the other is somewhat behind. Since Al and Laura Ries are a father-and-daughter team, they do not have a full partnership of equals because Laura started out as an apprentice to Al and is still somewhat his junior. However, Laura has been contributing and taking on more as time goes on.

Author 101 Advice

Collaborations with celebrities, experts, and business leaders can be difficult because they are frequently used to getting their way, and they may not devote the necessary time to the book. Even if you're equal partners on paper, they may feel that it's their book, that they're in charge, and that you're just working for them. Usually they're correct, and it may be best to accept it.

Experts often understand problems so well that they can't clearly explain them to others. They assume that everyone is on their level or they are so accustomed to speaking at a certain level that they go over other people's heads. When this occurs, their collaborators have to work hard to draw them out and make sure that they understand that the readers may not be at their level of understanding.

In addition, collaborators may have agreed to do X, Y, and Z but never come through and deliver as promised. They may mean well and actually intend to deliver, but somehow something came up to make it impossible. If you encounter this problem with your collaborator, you may have to do his or her share of the work if you want to complete the book. However, problems may arise that you can't solve. They may involve people you can't reach or information that you can't get on your own. So you have to wait, keep your fingers crossed, and hope that your collaborator will eventually produce.

Don't expect your collaborator to want the same benefits from the book as you do, but be careful that he or she doesn't want something that conflicts with your values or your best interests. Collaborators often have hidden agendas, which may be difficult to detect. If you get the slightest indication of potential problems, hash it out before you join forces, and include a provision in your agreement to deal with and settle disputes that may arise.

Working Together

Collaborations can be complex and difficult relationships, but they can also be wonderful, joyful, and highly fulfilling experiences, in which you learn, grow, and advance your career. In collaboration, you can build close personal relationships with remarkable individuals that can last for the rest of your life.

It's essential for collaborators to establish open, honest dialogues so that they communicate fully about the direction of the book, its content, and their work on it. Frequent discussions can help collaborators avoid misunderstandings and help them establish a smooth, productive working relationship. The smallest miscommunication can create problems such as sending collaborators off in different directions.

Before Vikki Weiss and Jennifer Block wrote *What to Do When You're Dating a Jew* (Three Rivers Press, 2000), they identified authors who had the quick, snappy tone that they wanted in their book. Then they split up chapters and each wrote a draft of a different chapter, which they exchanged and reviewed. After each review, they met and rewrote the chapter together word for word, to make sure that the book had a consistent tone. They tested their writing by continually reading it aloud until they knew it had the right voice.

Al and Laura Ries discuss each chapter thoroughly before they work on it to agree on exactly what the chapter should say. Just talking about it out loud helps. Verbalizing clears their ideas and usually gives them a blueprint to follow. When they agree on an approach, each of them can write his or her respective chapters and critique each other's drafts.

To enjoy a successful collaboration, keep the following in mind:

- From the outset, be open and honest; build a relationship in which both of you are dedicated to producing a fabulous book. Lay out your cards; explain precisely to potential collaborators what you want from this project and why you're getting involved, and find out what's in it for them. When each of you knows the other's objectives, it can help each of you succeed.

- Before you agree to work together, discuss each of your visions for the book. Explain how you see the book: its style, format, voice, and approach. Identify all of the resources and effort it will take to write the book. List the tasks to be completed and the steps involved. Then decide how each of them will be attacked and by whom. Find existing books with qualities you like or dislike, to use as examples of what you want or wish to avoid. Make sure you understand each other's likes and dislikes.

- Put it in writing. Even if you don't go to a lawyer and sign a collaboration agreement, discuss what each of you agrees to do and put it on paper. When your book is sold, you will enter into a contract with the publisher that outlines your book deal, and this writing will serve to clarify your arrangement with your collaborator. See the following chapter for a more detailed discussion of collaboration agreements.

- Discuss any concerns, doubts, and problems that you foresee. Talking about issues up front can frequently defuse them. And if your fears are reasonable, discussing them may help you plan together how to avoid or minimize them.

- Create a plan for how you will work together. Will you meet regularly in person, talk by phone, and/or communicate via email? If so, how often, for how long, and when? How will you exchange and review materials? What editing conventions will you use?

- Agree on a problem-solving mechanism to settle disputes. To resolve problems quickly, consider taking irresolvable differences to an objective third party whom you both trust and respect, such as your agent or attorney.

- As you work together, think of yourself as part of a team and put the needs of the team, or in this case, the book, before your own. In collaboration, your primary obligation should be to successfully complete the project, and doing so should come before your own objectives.

- Don't try to control your collaborator, because if you do, you will probably alienate him or her. Be open, fair, and willing to listen and compromise. Try to understand your collaborator's position. Be flexible. If your partner feels strongly and says, "I don't like that," cut it and move on.

- Be a reasonable and pleasant collaborator. Ease your criticism of your partner, control your temper and ego, and always try to do what's best for the book. When disputes arise, think primarily about the good of the book even though it may conflict with what's best for you. Take the position that your day will come.

- Try to blend your voices so that it will be impossible for either you or your collaborator to tell who wrote what. After a while, your collaborative efforts may take on a separate voice, one that isn't yours or your collaborator's, but is something new and distinct.

My Least Favorite Part

The least favorite part of the writing process for Jean-Noel Bassior is when she feels overwhelmed by research. Even though she has a great organizational system, she feels at times that she is standing at the bottom of a towering mountain of research that is suddenly going to fall and inundate her. "When that occurs," Bassior suggests, "you have to step back or walk away to take a different perspective so you can get a grip on the situation."

Anatomy of a Collaboration

Collins Hemingway, who had collaborated with Bill Gates on *Business @ the Speed of Thought*, was hired to write *What's Right with America's Corporations* (Rodale, 2006) for Dr. Dan Baker and Dr. Cathy Greenberg after the project was under way. To start, Baker and Greenberg sent Hemingway a box of research materials and writing. Hemingway reviewed the materials and read the chapters they had drafted and their book proposal. He concentrated on their outline and did some reading on his own, including Baker's book *What Happy People Know* (St. Martin's Griffin, 2004).

After he read the initial materials, Hemingway conducted research to obtain missing information and shape the book's organization. Normally, he would have preferred to conduct all the research up front, but since this project was in process, he had to discover what the book was about while he was writing it.

Hemingway, Baker, and Greenberg then held three two-day, face-to-face meetings in Tucson, where they went over the project from beginning to end several times. Hemingway asked questions and Baker and Greenberg gave him information. For example, Baker and Greenberg spoke about the fear and flight response, so Hemingway asked them to give him an example of a typical flight response in a business setting. He let them answer and then tried to flesh out their responses. Then they would kick ideas around, and from that, certain trends and additional ideas would emerge. Hemingway taped the sessions and took extensive notes.

The face-to-face meetings helped Hemingway understand how Baker and Greenberg thought, where they were coming from, and what they wanted to achieve. It also showed him the structure and flow that they wanted in the book. Hemingway realized that in order to capture those elements in the book, it was more important for him to understand them and what they wanted rather than to just incorporate particular phrases they used.

"You have to understand how people think and identify their objectives before you can fully understand it from their perspective and communicate it to others," Hemingway explains. "It's important for the book to reflect how they approach issues, how they think and process information. It puts the information they gave me in their context and shows me the direction that I should follow to construct the book. Then a lot of the development can come from my own head and I only need to bounce things off them and have them fill in."

When Hemingway works with clients, he records their conversation. He usually listens to the tapes and transcribes only those he thinks could be helpful. Generally, he prefers to rely on his notes because he thinks they really capture what is most important. He may not refer to transcripts of the recordings if the book is developing in an interesting way, in order to give it the room and freedom to continue. In most cases, he uses the transcripts as backups for his notes and to get an emotional and psychological sense rather than a literal rendering.

For example, Hemingway worked with a client who spoke in visual images, so Hemingway was forced to review his tapes to capture the client's exact words. Then, he had to learn how to translate the client's images to language that readers could readily understand. Baker and Greenberg spoke conceptually, in terms of ideas; so, Hemingway had to learn to understand their ideas in order to explain them. He just couldn't use their exact words, which most readers wouldn't understand. Then he had to find examples that illustrated those thoughts. As he did, it stimulated Baker and Greenberg to come up with their own examples or variations of Hemingway's examples, which added life to the book.

After meeting with Baker and Greenberg, Hemingway would return to his home and write about the information he received. He then held weekly phone conversations with his clients, which ran for an hour to an hour and a half. After their sessions, he would compose drafts and submit them to his clients. Baker and Greenberg would review his drafts, comment on them, pass them back and forth, and send them back to Hemingway.

Hemingway feels that his greatest value to a collaborative project is his ability and willingness to contribute his life experience. For example, he has thirty years' experience in business, so he knows business examples that can illustrate his clients' points. Often, these examples broaden or extend points his clients want to stress. Hemingway's business and life experience give his books a special advantage, he believes.

As an experienced, professional writer, Hemingway knows writing, books, and publishing. He knows what is entailed in writing and producing an entire book. He understands how complex material should be structured, worded, and presented, how to conduct interviews and deal with editors and publishing personnel.

Hemingway's overall collaboration plan was to work from Baker and Greenberg's table of contents, conduct the basic research, and call his clients when he got stuck. When he called, they usually gave him information or pointed him to places where he could find what he needed. At other times, they weren't available when he needed them, so Hemingway found it easier to just get the material himself, which frequently helped him get a better understanding of the subject.

"I had to understand on a deep level exactly what they were trying to say and then write it at a more simplified level to make sure that readers could understand and follow it," Hemingway revealed. He also had to put their theories into practical business applications or situations that readers would relate to and understand.

Action Items

1. Name three situations in which you might need to collaborate on a book.
2. What are the two major drawbacks to collaboration?
3. List seven questions that you would ask people who refer you to possible collaborators.
4. List seven questions that you would ask potential collaborators.
5. Why is it important for collaborators to speak with one another before they agree to work on a book project?

·············· **REMEMBER** ··············

Need versus desire. Collaboration may be the only way to get your book written and published if you don't have the time, writing talent, or necessary credentials. Determine precisely what you want from a collaborator and then contact people who are involved with books and writing, such as agents and writers, for recommendations.

Be ready to work it out. When you collaborate on a book project, you form a partnership, and like all such relationships, difficulties can arise. Try to find out all you can about possible collaborators before you agree to work with them.

Meet with them and speak with them personally. Question them thoroughly and make sure that you are clear about how you envision the book and what you want from them.

Chapter 12

....

COLLABORATION:
THE LEGAL IMPLICATIONS

....

The profession of book writing makes horse racing seem like a solid, stable business.
—John Steinbeck

This chapter covers:

- Frequent scenarios
- Dispute resolution
- Ghostwriters

Note: The information that follows in this chapter is provided in this book solely to alert you to some of the legal problems that may arise from book collaborations. It is specifically *not* intended to give you legal advice. If problems occur regarding book or writing collaborations, obtain the advice of an attorney![1]*

Book collaborations may not work for any number of reasons, and the collaborators may decide to go their separate ways. Dissolving the relationship could be complicated and may involve many sticky legal issues, including who owns and has the right to use writing that has been completed and what financial obligations exist.

Collaborations are business relationships that can have serious legal implications. So, before you begin to work with a collaborator, consult with an attorney regarding the preparation of a collaboration agreement that will define in writing the duties and responsibilities of the parties and their financial arrangement.

In any collaboration, it's essential for the collaborators to understand exactly what they're expected to do and what they will receive for doing it. When collaborators see their duties and responsibilities in black and white, it will increase the chances that the collaboration will run more smoothly.

Frequent Scenarios

Like marriages, most collaborations begin optimistically. At first, the parties give little thought to the fact that problems could arise and the legal consequences that may ensue. Everyone is all wrapped up in the excitement of the book and focused on bringing it to life. "What begins informally can result in great disappointment, despair and disruption," attorney Lloyd J. Jassin advises. "So address the issues—such as cash or compensation, credit and control—up front in a written collaboration agreement."

Unfortunately, problems can arise in any collaboration. Common scenarios include:

---

1   *We would like to express our thanks and great appreciation to Lloyd J. Jassin, Esq. (*www.copylaw.com*), a New York City attorney who specializes in publishing law, for his help and guidance with this chapter. Jassin is coauthor of *The Copyright Permission and Libel Handbook: A Step-by-Step Guide for Writers, Editors, and Publishers* (Wiley Books for Writers Series, 1998).

1. One of the collaborators feels that he or she is doing the bulk of the work while the other isn't producing as promised. Frequently, this scenario occurs in collaborations with celebrities or high-profile individuals. Often, they may have many other pressing and more important demands on their time. "It's human nature to believe that you're carrying more of the weight that your collaborator," Jassin observes. "Even in a good relationship, problems occur."

2. You collaborate with a partner in writing a book, and after you're well into the process, your partner decides that it's not in his or her interest to continue the project or publish the book. You have spent lots of time writing and you can't take your contribution and reuse it.

3. Collaborators such as ghostwriters often write book proposals before they enter into collaboration agreements. Often, they have agreed that when the book is sold, the ghostwriter will write the book. However, when the book is sold, the other party either reneges on the deal or wants the ghostwriter to sign an unreasonable or unfair agreement. If the ghost refuses, he or she will be left out in the cold, and the other party will hire another ghost to write the book. Although the ghost can always sue, the other parties are frequently celebrities or successful businesspeople who can outspend and financially wear down the ghostwriter.

4. You participate in a project with a group of other authors. The book is very successful, and every year, the publisher puts out a revised edition. Somewhere down the line, around the third or fourth edition, you and the other authors are receiving huge royalties, but one of your partners stops pulling his or her weight or is not contributing at all.

5. You're a photographer who has an idea for a photographic book. After you compile the shots you want to publish, you consult a friend who has written a number of books, regarding possible formats for the text that might accompany your photographs. After the book is published, your old friend claims to be entitled to coauthorship credit and threatens to sue unless he receives a share of the royalties and joint copyright ownership.

Rick Says

To address these and many other potentially difficult issues, see an attorney who is experienced with publishing contracts before you agree to collaborate. Experienced attorneys can anticipate most problems and draft agreements that can protect your interests. The time and money it can take may be well worth it.

Dispute Resolution

A collaboration agreement should specify that if a dispute arises that the parties cannot resolve by themselves, they will take it to be resolved by an objective party who they agree upon. That can be an attorney, literary agent, editor, or any individual they trust and feel will be fair and objective. The agreement should specify that the decision rendered would be final and binding on each of the parties.

Another option is submitting the dispute to either mediation or binding arbitration. In mediation, the dispute is usually brought before a single mediator who tries to come up with a resolution that the parties can accept. In mediation, there is no winner or loser and the objective of the proceeding is to work out the problem or dispute. Mediation decisions usually require each party to give and take, but the problems are usually resolved so that they can continue to work together. Although mediation isn't binding and the parties don't have to comply with the ruling, over 90 percent of mediation proceedings are successful.

Unlike mediation, arbitration is binding on the parties, and the courts will generally not consider matters that have been arbitrated. In arbitration, the parties go before an arbitrator or panel of arbitrators who rule on the dispute. Like litigation, arbitration produces a winner and a loser, and the objective is to resolve the dispute, not work it out. The advantage of arbitration is that it's usually quicker and less expensive than litigation or mediation.

My Favorite Part

Guy Kawasaki loves the editing process, when you go over your book again and again. However, he also hates the editing process. "It's very painful, but I'm a masochist," Kawasaki admits. "Editing is where you separate the men from the boys."

The problem with arbitration is that arbitrators don't have to follow the law, and arbitrators may not be experienced in publishing or copyright law. Therefore, Lloyd J. Jassin, Esq., recommends that collaboration agreements specify that the arbitrator be a publishing or entertainment attorney with at least six years' experience in practice.

Robyn Says

Even if you have a collaboration agreement, make every effort to get along well with your collaborator. It will make your project go more smoothly and be more fun. Don't threaten to take legal action when any little issue arises, but try to work out the dispute. The important thing is to figure out how the relationship will work before you begin the project. Get everything in writing and get it signed; make sure you fully understand what each of you is supposed to do. If disputes arise, right off the bat, it might indicate what the rest of the project will be like. So before you start the work, make sure that you really want to be in business with this person.

Ghostwriters

For writers, ghostwriting can be a viable alternative to publishing their own books. By ghostwriting, they can earn income, get authorship credits, and have strong samples of their work. However, a number of problems can arise in ghostwriting relationships. They include:

- **Lack of access.** A subject who hires a ghostwriter may be reluctant or unwilling to give the ghostwriter access to his or her friends and/or documents or to divulge critical information. After they agree to work together, the subject's contribution may be passive at best and zero at worst. So, the ghostwriter may end up doing the bulk or all of the work despite the author's promises.
- **Payment.** Although payment provisions differ, ghostwriters are usually entitled to a portion of their fee upon signing the collaboration agreement. Subsequent payments can be contingent on the subject's finding the ghost's writing is satisfactory in content and form at certain

milestones. For example, after a certain number of pages or chapters or a percentage of the book has been written. It can be a good idea to attach the book proposal to the agreement, or to at least reference it, in order to establish a standard under which the ghostwriter's performance can be judged.

- **Exclusivity.** Collaboration agreements should specify whether the ghostwriter is working exclusively for the subject or is also simultaneously working on other projects. Except for the largest and most high profile ghostwriting projects, most ghostwriters work on more than one project at a time. However, if projects demand their exclusive attention, the ghostwriting agreement should so specify.

- **Acknowledgment.** How a ghostwriter will be acknowledged can be another important issue. Will it be on the cover, the title page, or nowhere at all? Will the ghost be credited in the book as a coauthor, by "as told to," or "with"? When subjects negotiate that they are to be credited as the sole author, they often agree to thank the ghostwriter for his or her contributions in the book's acknowledgements. They also frequently give the ghostwriter the right to disclose that he or she was the ghostwriter on the book.

- **Use of material.** Authors have different views on how ghostwriters should be permitted to use material that they gather or write for a book. That's why it's so important to sign a collaboration agreement before you start working on a project. Some authors are happy to allow ghostwriters to use material from the book or portions of it in his or her portfolio, but others require ghostwriters to first get their permission.

- **Authorship credit.** Again, procedures differ and are always negotiable. The names of some ghostwriters appear on book covers or title pages— for example, Mark Steisel is listed on the title page of this book. Other books state "as told to" or "with," and then give the ghostwriter's name. Ghostwriters may not be credited anywhere or may be mentioned only in the book's acknowledgments, which is why they're called ghostwriters. It all depends on the arrangements the parties reach.

- **Expenses.** Some ghostwriting projects involve significant expenses for travel, interviews, materials, and equipment. When substantial expenses are anticipated, a fund should be set up for large-ticket items. If expenses are to be reimbursed, the subject should place a ceiling on the amount that the ghostwriter can spend without first obtaining his or her approval. However, these details should be agreed upon in writing since every situation differs.

- **Nondisclosure.** Subjects may wish to prevent a ghostwriter from disclosing information in the book prior to publication or information that the ghost receives or is told that is not included in or is deleted from the book. They may also require the ghostwriter to agree not to discuss or reveal information about them at any time and for any reason.

- **Representations and warranties.** Ghostwriters should represent and warrant that they are available and will provide their writing services on a priority basis. The idea is to convey that the ghostwriter does not have commitments that will materially conflict with his or her ability to write the subject's book. If ghostwriters provide representations and warranties about the accuracy of and right to use information in the book, material provided by the subject should be excluded. If that information infringes or violates anyone's rights, the ghostwriter should not be subject to liability. These exclusions should apply to the rights of privacy and publicity.

- **Inability to complete.** Provisions should be included in ghostwriting agreements that govern what happens if the ghostwriter is unable to complete the project. If the ghostwriter becomes disabled or dies before the publisher accepts the manuscript, a provision should be written that he, she, or his or her survivors will be entitled to an amount in direct proportion to the work completed. The amount of advances or monies paid to the ghostwriter should also be factored in. The provision should also control how or if the ghostwriter will be credited for the work completed.

My Least Favorite Part

Revision is David Fryxell's least favorite part of a book-writing project. "Revision is hard," Fryxell points out. "And revision where you have to cut is excruciating."

Action Items

1. Describe three scenarios for which a collaboration agreement could be helpful.
2. How could a dispute resolution provision in a collaboration agreement work?
3. Name four issues that could be covered in a collaboration agreement with a ghostwriter.
4. What rights should a ghostwriter have to the materials he or she wrote for a book project?
5. What does a nondisclosure provision in a collaboration agreement cover?

·················· **REMEMBER** ··················

Legally briefed. When you collaborate on a book, you are entering into a relationship that can have serious legal implications. So, before you begin to work with a collaborator, consult with an attorney and consider having a written collaboration agreement prepared. A collaboration agreement will set forth all parties' duties and responsibilities, which should increase the odds that the collaboration will run more smoothly.

Spell it out. Issues that should be covered in collaboration agreements include how disputes should be resolved, the financial understanding of the parties, and how each of the parties will be acknowledged. In addition, agreements can cover the collaborators' right of access to people and information, exclusivity, use of materials, representations and warranties, and inability to complete.

Chapter 13

······································

TIPS: THE TOP TWENTY

······································

Language is the blood of the soul into which
thoughts run and out of which they grow.
—Oliver Wendell Holmes

We asked the authors we interviewed for this book what tips they would give aspiring authors, and they were extremely forthcoming. In fact, they gave us more tips than we could include in this chapter. Many of their suggestions have already been included in this book, but we have repeated some because we consider them so important.

The top twenty tips that authors offered are set forth below. They are not presented in any particular order. They are:

1. **Write with passion.** To be a great writer, you must be passionate about what you write, because your feelings come across in your writing and in how you promote your book. Passion is a driving force. It will make you want to learn about your subject, and it will breathe life and fire into your words. Passion is also a major ingredient that readers take from books; it inspires them and makes them open their minds to the ideas and information your book contains. When you present your book idea to agents and editors, they look for passion because they know that authors' enthusiasm and belief in their writing will drive them to make their books successful. Writing is hard work, and if you're not passionate, the writing process can become even more difficult and the chances of success less. Write from your heart.

Childhood Passions

Many of the authors we interviewed have written about subjects that they were passionate about as children. For example, they have written about movies and movie stars, television programs, and sports. These authors found that over the years, they acquired massive knowledge about their passions and a burning desire to learn more. They took great pride in their knowledge and special pleasure in sharing it with others. When they told people about their passions, they were frequently showered with terrific leads and helpful information.

2. **If you don't love the act of writing, consider having someone else do it.** Trying to write when you don't like to write is torture. Plus, your feelings about writing will come through. It's usually much smarter and more successful to collaborate with a writer. Your decision to write a book may make sense from a marketing or career standpoint, but taking on projects that you don't like generally doesn't provide a good result or a good quality of life. However, some writers find that the status of being a published author helps them overcome the pain they endured in writing their books.

3. **Be disciplined.** Although writers thrive on, and can get swept away by, inspiration, those moments may be elusive and hard to find. Inspiration is the spark, but it takes work to build that spark into the fire that you need to write a book. So become disciplined; sit at the computer every day for a minimum amount of time and write. Some days, your writing will just flow smoothly, you can't type fast enough to capture all the words and ideas; you won't be able to stop. At other times, you may not be able to write a single word. However, that's okay because it's how the writing process works. Some days are productive while other days are bone dry. The important thing is to write continually. Start by setting writing goals for how many hours a day you're going to write or how many pages you want to turn out. Experiment and try to find what works for you, and when you do, keep at it.

4. **Take on projects that stimulate you and push you in exciting new ways.** Don't pick topics or styles just because they're easy or expected of you; they usually won't show you at your best. Try to avoid repeating yourself, which can be difficult because people frequently want what you've demonstrated that you can do well. However, repetition can be deadly because it can eliminate the passion and curiosity that make books great. It's also hard creatively to find new ways to cover well-traveled ground. Repetition can also bore you, so push yourself further, explore your limits, and take on something new.

5. **Early on, develop a thick, entrepreneurial skin with regard to writing.** If you get one rejection, don't give up. Don't consider a form letter, which is frequently unsigned, to be the ultimate judgment on not only the one piece of writing that you submitted, but also on your ability to write in general. Don't let it prevent you from submitting anything else again. Keep in mind that editors and publishers have a limited number of slots to fill. You may give them the hottest book ever, but if it doesn't fit a particular slot, they will reject it. However, another publisher may love it and the books that you subsequently submit.

6. **You can't go with anyone else's writing schedule or approach.** We all differ; some of us write well in the morning, others do best later in the day. Some wait until the very last minute and then hold

writing marathons where they turn out their entire book in record time. Discover your own pace and how, when, and where you work best. If you're a crammer who needs the pressure of waiting until the bitter end, go with what works for you. It's the quality of your product that counts, not the manufacturing process. It's crucial to find your own speed, and while you're at it, make sure to inject a large dose of enjoyment into it.

7. **The gatekeepers who work in publishing may have little imagination.** Many of them may not necessarily want brilliant, innovative ideas. They may just want more commercial books that they believe will sell. Even if they are captivated by your ideas and approaches, their houses or boards still may say no. At publishing houses, gatekeepers generally look for just a few basic things, the most important being books that they think will sell. So make sure that your proposal is well written, presents your book idea clearly, justifies the market, and shows how your book is unique because that's what gatekeepers want. They also tend to copy a lot; they want to get on the bandwagon of trends and developments that have been successful.

8. **Be cooperative, meet every deadline, be easy to work with, and promptly do what is asked; in fact, when possible, do more.** Publishers have an endless number of writers they can publish, so if you're good to work with and make their job easier, they will want to work with you. However, if you're difficult and create additional work for them, they may turn elsewhere. Don't be a difficult or demanding prima donna because the word will get out and editors and publishers won't want to work with you.

9. **Be accessible.** Think in the long term and build your reputation and your career. Answer all of your email; be friendly and helpful. People will spread the word, and word of mouth is essential in building writing careers. When people email to tell you that they loved your book, thank them for their kind words. Keep track of their email and postal addresses. Ask if you can send them your newsletter of information about you and your upcoming appearances, ventures, or books. If they give you special praise, ask if they would be willing to write a review of your book on

the online bookseller sites. Provide them with the link. If you become successful, help other writers.

10. **Write nonfiction that is as exciting and as alive as fiction.** Study fiction and incorporate elements of novels and mysteries into your books. Be daring; create scenes, dramatic situations, and suspense. Use vivid stories as examples, spice up your descriptions to make them more memorable, and use dialogue. Play with the order of your chapters, but be sure not to destroy your book's logic so you continue to keep your readers engaged.

11. **Look at the bigger picture, not just in terms of this one book.** Assess the needs of the marketplace regarding how big your book can be, create a large vision around it, and don't let the book just be a book. Create other opportunities to generate excitement around the book, like special events, a curriculum, newsletters, speaking engagements, workshops, seminars, and products. Learn your craft and organize the marketplace around what you do.

12. **Produce top-quality books, nothing less.** Quality is what will make you unique and set you apart. Set high standards and always meet them. Take pride in your work, and if it's not top quality and will not help others, consider not publishing it until it is. Make your book a complete package that delivers excellence all around. Conduct research on how other books are written, structured, and designed. Work at the highest level to distinguish yourself from the rest of the crowd.

13. **Keep at it and persevere.** It doesn't make any difference how many rejections you get, because all it takes is one acceptance for your book to be published. If your book or proposal is rejected, remember that publishers need authors. They have a steady pipeline to fill, so they need books and authors to produce the products they sell. The book proposal that you submit today may not be what they want, but the proposal you send next could hit the bull's-eye.

14. **Don't try to write the perfect first draft.** Instead, concentrate on just getting information down. Be prepared to write multiple drafts, and don't worry about how rough your initial draft is—you can always refine it. Your number-one priority should be to capture, and not lose, your ideas. When you see a blank page, fill it up. Don't worry if it doesn't

make sense—keep writing until you can't go any further, because you can always come back and clean it up.

15. **When you're writing, don't read books by your direct competitors in the genre in which you're writing.** Read every other book on the planet, but not those on the same subject. Reading your competitors, especially those who write well, can be intimidating and can cloud your thinking. Don't compare your writing to that of others. Writers informed us that when they read their competitors, their competitors' styles and approaches often influenced and intimidated them. Since writers have different styles and approaches, reading other authors can pull you away from your own style and what you do best.

16. **Don't try to be all things to all people.** It's usually better for a book to address specific readers than to try to cover the entire world. Books on leadership, for example, do better than general books. A book on how seniors can get jobs can do better than a comprehensive manual that covers every single career stage and topic. Know your particular niche, identify your precise audience, and focus on addressing and providing benefits to them.

17. **Don't take yourself too seriously, or it will come through in your writing.** Too many authors come across like they're talking down to their readers, and they give the impression that they're smarter than those who read their books. Readers can quickly sense it, and they resent it. It can ruin your career.

18. **Find a supportive individual for your writing.** Choose someone other than a member of your immediate family. All writers need a cheerleader, someone who supports and believes in their writing. As a writer, you will face bruising times, times of depression and lack of belief in yourself, no matter how much you've written. At such times, you need people to encourage you and tell you that you can do it so you can continue to push on.

19. **Reward yourself for your accomplishments.** Enjoy what you have completed, and when you reach certain milestones, such as completing your first draft and submitting your book, acknowledge your effort and success. Celebrate by doing something special, like going for a wonderful

meal, getting a massage, or visiting with dear friends. Writing can be a lonely activity, so find ways to say thank you to yourself and enjoy what you achieved.

20. **Believe in the success and salability of your book, and keep trying to make it better.** Stick with your conviction during all rejections and obstacles that you face. Continue to believe because if you do, it's hard to give up. Perseverance is essential, even after publishers repeatedly say no. When they say no, think what else you can provide, what you can do better. Specifically, ask how you can improve your chances of getting your book published and make the changes they suggest.

Chapter 14

....

MISTAKES: THE TOP TWENTY

....

A writer is a person for whom writing is more difficult than it is for other people.
—Thomas Mann

We also asked the authors who we interviewed for this book what they felt were the most common and serious mistakes that authors in their genre make. The top twenty tips that they offered are set forth below. Again, they are not listed in any particular order. They are:

1. **In many books, authors don't clearly state what the problem is and are much too eager to get to their solutions.** As a result, they make their important points too early, saying everything they have to say by page 50. Therefore, they end up repeating the same points throughout

the remainder of the book. By not fully discussing the problem, they put themselves in a position where they have nowhere else to go.

2. **Writers should try to avoid being salespeople in their books.** They should provide ideas, information, and insights and not try to sell their books, because it will diminish the power of the material they provide to readers. Essentially, readers want to know how to get information and solve problems. They don't need to hear a bunch of hype from you on how great and valuable your book will be to them. Publishers want authors who have credentials so they can convince readers that the authors are qualified to write their books. However, they don't want you to come off like a shill or a pitchman for yourself or your products.

3. **In the rush to write books, many writers don't think through whether they really want to spend the time it will take to write a book on their topic.** Frequently, all they know is that they want to write a book, and they seize on the first subject that they might know or think they can write a book about. Since writing a book is a major undertaking that can take years, writers must be truly fascinated by their topics or the process will go very slowly and probably painfully regardless of how much money it might earn.

4. **Writing can be a very personal matter, so be careful whom you speak with about your writing.** Don't share your ideas, information, or plans indiscriminately or with people who don't understand what the creative process entails, because they can be unduly critical and discouraging. Although their criticism usually isn't valid because they don't understand what's involved in the creative process, it still can sting. It can destroy your confidence and set you back, especially when the criticism is from people whom you respect.

5. **Authors frequently make the mistake of making their books too theoretical.** They think that as authors they have to show that they're authorities on their subjects. So they include too much data and try too hard to prove that they're experts. What actually occurs is the opposite; they show that they are only theorists, talking heads. In a similar vein, authors often include too much jargon and technical language in their

books, which confuses readers and does not facilitate communication and understanding.

6. **Writers often don't know where to start.** When they have a narrative or a time thread, many start at the wrong point; they may give too much background or not enough to prime the pump. And their starting point may not be very interesting. For example, opening a biography with the subject's birth may be a logical place to begin, but it is seldom the best way to grab readers' attention. Writers also have problems regarding where to end. If you can solve where to start and where to end, most of the other writing will come together. Try to start with a bang; grab readers from the start because otherwise they may not stick around.

7. **Not planning.** Having a road map for your book is essential; begin with a solid idea of where you want to go and how you hope to get there. Planning helps you make your writing more interesting, it keeps you from wandering and helps you stay on course. Planning makes it easier for you to write the book because it gives you a diagram that you can follow and helps you make sure that you get everything in. Although you may stray from your plan, it helps you to remain organized and focused.

8. **Writers mistakenly believe that a top-quality book and a great publisher are all that matters.** What matters most is that they have a compelling idea and an audience that wants or needs to learn about that idea. Writers have many options today in addition to traditional publishers. Being published by a traditional publisher, even a well-respected, major house, may not be as effective in reaching your core demographic as self-publishing and running your own tightly focused publicity campaign.

9. **Writers often have unrealistic expectations.** Instead of establishing themselves as published authors and building from there, many aspiring writers insist on making a big initial splash. They seek large advances, which effectively kills the chances of their books being published. Some believe that they deserve large rewards for all the hard work they have done, and sometimes they're just greedy, stupid, or impatient. While it's

important to be confident and believe in your book, thinking that it will be a best seller is unrealistic; the odds are about twenty thousand to one.

10. **Too many writers want to publish books for the wrong reasons.** They want to publish to advance their careers or boost their egos, not because they have an important message to deliver. Instead of caring about what their books can provide and how they will help others, they care only about what they will get. Authors should ask, "Does my book serve a need in the marketplace?" If you write to serve, you will probably be more successful.

11. **Inexperienced writers often wrestle with impatience.** They frequently mistakenly expect to simply sit at the computer and dash out books lickety-split; experienced authors know better. Overnight success is a dream; writing a book takes time, lots of time. Before you start a book project, learn about the process and what it entails so you understand what you will be required to do and just how long it can take. Otherwise, you will be in for a big disappointment.

12. **Writers are often uncertain or mistaken about who their readers will be.** To communicate effectively, authors must speak directly to their audiences, which is difficult or impossible when they don't know who they are. Writers frequently overestimate the size of their audiences and try to address everyone. Unfortunately, in doing so, they frequently don't clearly and convincingly communicate to anyone. Know exactly who your target readers are and zero in on them. Start by identifying who will be most interested and then include others who might be interested.

13. **Many writers do not understand the market.** Writers must understand the market for the types of books they hope to write. Certain books don't sell many copies, and it may not make sense to write a title that addresses only a small audience. In learning about the market, writers will be alerted to the publishers that may be willing to publish their books, publishers who have published titles on their subjects. It also helps to know what similar works are on the market.

14. **Too many writers get enamored with subjects and think that there is more to them than there actually is.** So, they try to expand a limited idea into enough material to fill a book by padding, repeating, and over

explaining. The old sales technique of repeating information to make sure that it sinks in doesn't work with books because repetition becomes irritating. It may make readers think that you feel they're not intelligent. In nonfiction books, unnecessary repetition can be the enemy because it can make readers turn off. They mentally stop paying attention.

15. **Lack of dialogue and questions can make for a dry read.** Readers enjoy hearing from characters. They like reading how they speak and put their thoughts together. Nonfiction books that are all gray text without any characters or dialogue can be boring. Most of the good nonfiction writers treat nonfiction as fiction by using characters, dialogue, and scenes. Material in nonfiction can be as astonishing, if not more astonishing, than anything you read in fiction, so why not write it that way?

16. **Sentences and paragraphs that are longer than readers can digest will make readers put down books.** Some authors get overly technical in order to prove how much they know. They write about things they know and their readers don't know, but they write as if their readers are on the same wavelength as they are. You have to bring your readers along gently. Realize that although you may have been working with this material for years, it may be your readers' first exposure to it. "Act as if you're climbing a mountain with your readers," Jay Conrad Levinson recommends. "You go first and lead, but offer them your hand to bring them to your level. You set the pace, but don't make it too fast for your readers to keep up. Many writers go too fast and don't cover basic points that their readers need to proceed."

17. **Writers often believe that they must include every one of their thoughts, all of their brilliant gems.** They want to include every idea and sentence that they have fondness for in spite of the fact that it may not have much to do with the key points in the book. Including so much, especially when it's not directly on target, can suffocate their most important points. It's overkill that obscures their writing and confuses readers. It takes up valuable space that could have been used better.

18. **Authors frequently use the improper level and tone of writing for their readers.** To communicate effectively, you must address your real

audience, not the audience you would like to be writing for. If you're an academic who is trying to write for the masses, you can't insist on documenting every point you make. Instead, be conversational and try to simply communicate with your readers on the level that they can easily understand.

19. **Young writers tend to try to throw all of their good stuff into their first book, even when it doesn't really fit.** They hold nothing back. If they want to build writing careers and not just be one-shot successes, they must pace themselves so they can build on their initial publications with books that are equally strong or even stronger. Trust that you will have other great ideas and that some of your current ideas will find other uses or be in your next book.

20. **Many writers are overly self-critical and it paralyzes them.** They torment themselves over every word and line, which makes the writing experience painful and unsatisfying. Such pain always reveals itself in writing. While it is good to be self-critical during the editing process, it can be counterproductive during the creative phase. Don't hold yourself to impossible standards. Develop your own standards, and don't impose other writers' standards on yourself.

Chapter 15

SUMMING UP

If you're going through hell, keep going.
—Winston Churchill

Congratulations on completing this book! We've enjoyed writing it, and we sincerely hope that it will be beneficial to you. We also thank those of you who have read our other Author 101 books.

No one can become an author overnight—it takes months and years of hard work and tenacity and loads of resources. But in the end, it's definitely worth the effort. Being published authors is terrific; we've loved it, and we hope that this book will give you information and insights that will help you join the ranks. Being authors has significantly enriched our lives, and we know it will do the same for you.

Before we end this book and say adieu, we would like to add a few final words to help you on your way.

Writing is an emotionally driven pursuit. Much of what comes out depends on what's in you. How you feel, your state of mind, and the depth of your passion will strongly influence what you write and whether your book is ultimately published. Whether authors succeed or fail can be as attributable to their attitudes as to their talents—even more so. To succeed, writers must truly believe in themselves, be totally convinced that have something important to say, and be determined to write and publish their books. They must be their own best advocates, taskmasters, and supporters.

When your book idea is turned down or you're told that your book is not worth publishing, don't let it stop you. Instead, regroup. If you have a burning desire to write your book, do everything to make it happen. Rewrite, revamp, and refocus—do whatever it takes. Listen to your critics, consider their comments, but don't give up. If you want to become an author badly enough, your time will probably come.

At every stage of the writing and publishing process, determination is crucial. Writers must come up with great book ideas, find the right direction and voice for those ideas, complete lots of hard work, and navigate their way through the mysterious book-publishing industry. They must overcome obstacles and setbacks and withstand criticism and rejections all along the way. And frequently, they must do it alone.

Good writing, like most skills, takes time to develop, which means that most writers must continually write. They must practice, learn, and refine their work. Then they must get it out there for others to see—and critique.

Sadly, many aspiring writers get discouraged when they run into difficulties or when their writing isn't praised. So they quit, never to try again. As a result, all their hopes for their books, all the promise, all the good ideas that could have helped others may vanish and not be shared.

Don't give up.

Be strong, patient, and willing to learn, and don't give up. Be prepared for the difficulties you will probably encounter and be determined to see it through. Ask yourself, were you able to ride a bicycle the first time you tried? Did you struggle and fall? But did you also get back up and keep trying until you got the hang of it? And did riding soon become second nature to you, something you did with ease and can still do now?

Well, the same process, dedication, and determination must be applied if you want to write a book. Even if you have a great book idea and you write wonderfully, your first efforts may not be publishable, but that's no reason to quit. In fact, it's a great reason to continue, to keep trying to make your writing better and to master the craft.

Writing is a cumulative process: words make up sentences, sentences build into paragraphs, paragraphs become chapters, and chapters form books. Learning to be a successful writer follows the same cumulative path, but unfortunately, each step in learning is not as clearly defined as sentences, paragraphs, and chapters.

All your efforts and every attempt, setback, criticism, and rejection are building blocks for writing success. Each contains a lesson that can help teach you how to succeed. Together these lessons show you your mistakes, toughen your hide, help you understand the business, and direct you to the next level.

Pay close attention; understand the significance of each lesson and what it means. Make the necessary changes and adjustments to your writing, be patient, and persevere. Surround yourself with other supportive writers and work together to help each other succeed. The world needs another best-selling nonfiction book author, and with enough determination, talent, sweat, and persistence, it just might be you.

Thank you for reading this book and good luck!

ABOUT THE AUTHORS

RICK FRISHMAN is Publisher at Morgan James Publishing in New York and founder of Planned Television Arts (now called Media Connect), and has been one of the leading book publicists in America for over 37 years.

Rick works with many of the top book editors, literary agents, and publishers in America, including Simon and Schuster, Harper Collins and Random House.

He has worked with best-selling authors such as Mitch Albom, Bill Moyers, Stephen King, Caroline Kennedy, Howard Stern, President Jimmy Carter, Sophia Loren, Smokey Robinson, Nelson DeMille, Salmon Rushdie, John Grisham, Yogi Berra, Henry Kissinger, Jack Canfield, Alan Dershowitz, Arnold Palmer, Jackie Collins, Whoopi Goldberg, Gov. Mario Cuomo, and Senator John Glenn.

Morgan James Publishing publishes fiction and nonfiction books and by authors with a platform who believe in giving back. Morgan James gives a portion of every book sold to Habitat for Humanity.

Rick has also appeared on hundreds of radio shows and more than a dozen TV shows nationwide, including Oprah, Fox News and Bloomberg TV. He has also been featured in the *New York Times, Wall Street Journal, Associated Press, Selling Power Magazine, New York Post*, and scores of other publications.

He has appeared on stage with notables such as Sir Richard Branson, The Dalai Lama, T. Harv Eker, Jack Canfield, Mark Victor Hansen, Tony Hsieh, David Bach, Brian Tracy, Zig Ziglar and Brendon Burchard.

Rick is the coauthor of sixteen books, including national best-sellers *Guerrilla Publicity, Where's Your Wow, Guerrilla Marketing for Writers, The Expert Success Solution*, and *250 Rules of Business*. Rick's 15th book, *Networking Magic*-Second Edition was published in January of 2014. *Author 101: The Insider's Guide to Publishing* is Rick's 16th book.

Rick has a BFA in acting and directing and a BS in communications from Ithaca College. He is a sought-after lecturer on publishing and public relations and a member of PRSA and the National Speakers Association.

Rick and his wife Robbi live in Long Island, New York with their two Havanese puppies, Cody and Cooper. They have three children: Adam, Rachel, and Stephanie. www.rickfrishman.com

ROBYN SPIZMAN is one of the leading how-to, book-writing and gift experts in the country and a New York Times Best-selling author. A well-known seasoned media personality, Robyn has appeared often on television including repeatedly on the Today Show making holidays and special occasions memorable.

With over three decades of publishing successes and an expert publicist, she has written and co-authored dozens of books including the *Author 101* series and *Where's Your Wow? 16 Ways To Make Your Competitors Wish They Were You!* with Rick Frishman. She also teamed up with Tory Johnson and wrote books including *Take This Book To Work* about advancing your career along with books in the philanthropy world including *Don't Give Up, Don't Ever Give Up* based on the famous speech by Jimmy Valvano with her son, Justin Spizman, helping to raise money for the V Foundation for cancer research.

A prolific author, Robyn also authored *Make It Memorable: An A-Z Guide to Making Any Event, Gift or Occasion... Dazzling!, The*

Thank You Book, and ***When Words Matter Most***. Robyn's timely gift-giving tips and consumer suggestions have been heard around the country repeatedly on NBC's Today Show, CNN, MSNBC, CNNfn, Talk Back Live, Good Day New York, New York One, & numerous ABC, NBC, CBS and Fox affiliate stations. Her creative advice and books have been featured extensively in print media including *The New York Times, USA Today, USA Weekend, Women's Day, Ladies' Home Journal, Parade Magazine, Family Circle, Redbook, Cosmopolitan, Delta's Sky Magazine, Cosmo Girl, Parents Magazine, Better Homes and Gardens, Entrepreneur, Southern Living, Parade Magazine* and many other media outlets over the years.

Nominated for a Book for a Better Life Award, The USA Today Family Channel Award as well as Georgia's Author Of The Year, Business To Business Magazine named Robyn one of Atlanta's leading women and a Diva of Atlanta's business world. A popular keynote speaker, she has entertained audiences across the country with passionate and lively presentations on a variety of topics including the topic of giving and making a difference and other timely ideas. www.robynspizman.com

**The Premier Event for Marketing & Publishing Success
Expand your brand, your earnings and your reputation
as the authority in your field.**

After 3 days at Author 101 University you'll leave with the precise tools to propel yourself into the top 3% of any industry.

Sampling of some of the topics that will be shared with you:

- What you need to know to get a YES from agents & publishers
- Learn the secrets to becoming a best-selling author and sought-after speaker while growing your business revenue every quarter
- How to accomplish your goals rapidly without financial strain and pain, guided by mentors who have done it
- Understand how to master major media including books, radio, TV, and online media (social media, blogs-vlogs and more)
- How to get half a million dollars' worth of publicity for little or no money media (social media, blogs-vlogs and more)

What you'll Learn…

- How to create "hooks" for yourself and your business that will make you virtually irresistible to every media outlet and make coverage for yourself a virtual certainty.
- How to get rich and become famous by being a guest on radio shows without spending a dime on advertising.

- How to create promotional materials (media kits, etc.) that will have the media running to you for your opinion every time a story in your area pops up.
- How to quickly and easily create an automated process to capture leads and sales and to up-sell and cross-sell these people with a minimum of effort.
- How to make any book you write or publish an Amazon best seller with a system that has been PROVEN to work.

If you'd like to learn the secrets of getting your book published or how to turn your book or publishing business into a money machine, this course is for you. You'll get more out of this $497 seminar than any event this year offered at any price in the publishing industry. Check out our 100% money back guarantee!

Who is Eligible to Attend...
- Experts
- Entrepreneurs
- Authors
- Speakers
- Consultants
- You!

Why YOU should Attend...
Spend 3 days with Rick's close circle of experts, friends and mentors. His hand pick panel of literary agents want to meet you and read your proposal. The networking alone will change your life and business. Come be a part of our family. Held twice a year in October and March. **Reserve your spot now! www.author101.com**

Morgan James
The Entrepreneurial Publisher ™

Morgan James Publishing: The Entrepreneurial Publisher™ Helping Authors Grow Their Businesses.

Morgan James Publishing provides entrepreneurs with the vital information, inspiration and guidance they need to be successful. A division of Morgan James, LLC, Morgan James Publishing, The Entrepreneurial Publisher™, is recognized by Publishers Weekly as one of the nation's top publishers and is reported as being the future of publishing.

What we offer:
- Higher Author Royalties
- Book planning based on helping you maximize your brand and vision
- National distribution of your book
- A dedicated sales team to get your book placed
- Better discount on copies authors purchase (print cost plus a percentage)
- Enrollment in the Morgan James Speakers Group
- Small advances available

- Entrepreneurial Vision Mastermind with David Hancock, CEO of Morgan James, Publisher Rick Frishman, Publishing Director Jim Howard and Assistant Publishing Director Bethany Marshall to help you plan the book's strategy, including 20 hours of virtual assistant time to help you get started.
- Access to top thought leaders in public relations, membership web site development, and internet marketing
- Long-term thought leadership and strategy on a continual basis, you will have regular access to marketing strategists.

Visit MorganJamesPublishing.com to learn more. To see how we compare with others in the marketplace visit MorganJamesPublishing.com/compare

About Morgan James

Since its inception in 2003, Morgan James Publishing has grown from publishing six books per year to publishing 150 front list titles each year. With a backlist of over 2,000 titles and 20 *New York Times* bestseller listings, Morgan James Publishing can support and advise entrepreneurs through any challenge their business may face.

Morgan James Publishing was ranked on the Publisher's Weekly fast growing small press list for 3 years. *"Morgan James makes an extraordinary effort to help its authors to grow their own business."* PW's Lynn Andriani and Jim Milliot say.

Founded By David L. Hancock, with his bride, Susan. They named the new company after their two children, daughter Morgan Renee and son Ethan James. Morgan James counts many well-known authors in their author base, including Jay Conrad Levinson, Brendon Burchard, Jeff Walker, Joe Mechlinski, Gordon D'Angelo, Bill Glazer, Dan Kennedy, Jerry Colangelo, and Joe Vitale among others.